Long-term ill health, poverty and ethnicity

This publication can be provided in other formats, such as large print, Braille and audio.
Please contact:
Communications, Joseph Rowntree Foundation, The Homestead, 40 Water End, York YO30 6WP. Tel: 01904 615905. Email: info@jrf.org.uk

Long-term ill health, poverty and ethnicity

Sarah Salway, Lucinda Platt, Punita Chowbey, Kaveri Harriss
and Elizabeth Bayliss

 **JOSEPH ROWNTREE**
FOUNDATION

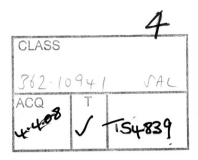
First published in Great Britain in 2007 by

The Policy Press
Fourth Floor, Beacon House
Queen's Road
Bristol BS8 1QU
UK

Tel no   +44 (0)117 331 4054
Fax no   +44 (0)117 331 4093
Email   tpp-info@bristol.ac.uk
www.policypress.org.uk

© University of Sheffield and University of Essex 2007

Published for the Joseph Rowntree Foundation by The Policy Press

ISBN 978 1 86134 993 4

British Library Cataloguing in Publication Data
A catalogue record for this book is available from the British Library.

Library of Congress Cataloging-in-Publication Data
A catalog record for this book has been requested.

Sarah Salway is Principal Research Fellow in the Centre for Health and Social Care Research, Sheffield Hallam University. **Lucinda Platt** is Senior Lecturer in Sociology in the Institute for Social and Economic Research, University of Essex. **Punita Chowbey** is a Research Associate in the School of Nursing and Midwifery, University of Sheffield. **Kaveri Harriss** is a doctoral student in the Centre for Population Studies, London School of Hygiene & Tropical Medicine. **Elizabeth Bayliss** is Executive Director at Social Action for Health.

The **Joseph Rowntree Foundation** has supported this project as part of its programme of research and innovative development projects, which it hopes will be of value to policy makers, practitioners and service users. The facts presented and views expressed in this report are, however, those of the authors and not necessarily those of the Foundation.

Cover design by Qube Design Associates, Bristol
Printed in Great Britain by Latimer Trend, Plymouth

Contents

List of tables, figures and boxes

Tables

Figures

Boxes

Acknowledgements

Numerous people have contributed to this piece of work. We would especially like to thank our team of community researchers for their hard work and insightful comments: Shareen Akhtar, Asma Akhter, Sam Amponsah, Scott Coleman, Wilma Cullen, Md. Enamul Haque, Amirul Islam, Evelynda Laryea, Malvinder Matharu, Arpana Rohatgi, Saleem Mallik and Shahid Yasin. We would also like to thank our advisory team members for their many useful suggestions and guidance: David Drew, Brian Fisher, Stephen Jenkins, Saffron Karlsen, Maura Farrelly, Sally Reeves, Tania Burchardt and Amanda McLeish. Helen Barnard at the Joseph Rowntree Foundation has also given important support to this project. We are indebted to a number of community-based organisations in London who helped us publicise our work and build positive relationships with local people, although in the interests of confidentiality we have decided not to name these organisations individually here. Amanda Baxter, Caroline Cross, Madhu Francine, Eyarun Chaudhury and Rizwan Rasheed provided expert transcription and translation support. Crown copyright material is reproduced with the permission of the Controller of HMSO and the Queen's Printer for Scotland. We are grateful to the Home Office for permission to use the 2001 Citizenship Survey and to the Office for National Statistics (ONS) for use of the Labour Force Survey. We are grateful to the UK Data Archive at the University of Essex for making the various datasets available. Neither ONS, the Home Office nor the Data Archive, however, bear any responsibility for the analysis or interpretation offered here. Finally, we thank all our respondents in the qualitative component of the study for so willingly giving their time and sharing their experiences. Clearly, this work would not have been possible without their valuable contribution.

Summary

Long-term health conditions affect a large proportion of working-age adults in Britain, often limiting daily activities, employment chances and incomes. This heavy burden of long-term ill health is now of major policy concern across the UK health and social welfare arenas. Government interventions aim to increase self-reliance among those with long-term ill health and reduce the costs to the state of such conditions. However, protecting individuals and families who experience long-term ill health against poverty is currently less subject to direct attention.

Research has highlighted the association between long-term ill health and the risk of poverty, and the far-reaching effects that such health conditions can have on individuals and their families. Less is known about the pathways that link ill health to poverty or how they may be broken. In particular, little attention has been given to social participation, access to non-labour income, and other knock-on effects. In Germany and the US the consequences of long-term ill health appear to be worse among minority ethnic groups, but little is understood about why this should be so, and these issues have not been examined in any detail for the UK.

The present study used a mixed-methods approach to explore the links between long-term ill health and dimensions of poverty across four ethnic 'groups': Bangladeshis, Pakistanis, White English (White British in the quantitative work) and Ghanaians (Black Africans in the quantitative work). Secondary analysis of national quantitative datasets (the Labour Force Survey and the Home Office Citizenship Survey) was combined with new detailed qualitative work (including locality-based rapid appraisal methods, 86 in-depth interviews and feedback workshops).

The study investigates: the ways in which family, community and wider society affect responses to long-term ill health (Chapter 2); the ways in which individuals adapt to having a long-term condition (Chapter 3); and the links between long-term ill health and employment (Chapter 4), access to welfare benefits (Chapter 5) and social participation (Chapter 6). The relevance of ethnicity is explored, although not assumed, across each of these areas.

The immediate family is shown to be the primary resource for managing the impact of long-term ill health across all groups. However, ethnic groups vary considerably in their levels of ill health and household composition, with important implications for the completion of tasks, including caring. Family members are often constrained in their ability to shift roles in response to ill health. Caring for children alongside an adult with long-term ill health can make paid work very difficult.

Positively adapting (developing 'resilience') in the face of ill health involves both mental adjustments and gaining control (coping strategies and experience). While some respondents showed remarkable buoyancy and enthusiasm for life, others were struggling and showed signs of serious emotional upset. Pressures to be 'normal' and hide ill health exist across all four ethnic groups, with negative implications for seeking healthcare and support. While holding on to prior roles and activities is positive for some, for others it leads to frustration and unhappiness. Achieving self-worth was particularly difficult for younger people with long-term conditions. Pakistani and Bangladeshi women also often struggled to feel valued. The close association with health services experienced by many respondents had discouraged a sense of control via: long delays to diagnosis/

treatment; lack of information and understanding; unpredictable symptoms; and frequent appointments. Few respondents received any support from external sources to positively adapt to their health condition.

Both minority ethnicity and long-term ill health are associated with greatly reduced chances of employment for men and women. Respondents with long-term ill health expressed a commitment to paid work and recognition of its benefits over and above income. However, there was variation in the extent to which paid work is seen as a possibility or priority. While there were differences in the ways in which relationships between paid work and ill health were discussed between the ethnic groups, quantitative analysis showed no ethnic differences in the effect of ill health on employment. Ethnic penalties in employment were, however, substantial and resulted in much lower rates of employment for those from the three minority groups, than among otherwise comparable White British men and women. Respondents identified diverse barriers to employment including: their inability following ill health to return to former types of employment (particularly that which was physically demanding); the demands of hospital appointments and the experience of chronic pain and fatigue; employers' inflexibility; and particularly for those with mental health conditions, stigma and discrimination. Pay was also adversely affected by having an activity-limiting health condition and by minority ethnicity.

Just 19% of those with an activity-limiting long-term condition received Disability Living Allowance. Pakistani, Bangladeshi and Black African individuals had much lower receipt than comparable White British. Our quantitative analyses also suggested striking differences in receipt of Incapacity Benefit by ethnicity, with White British men with activity-limiting conditions having the highest proportions in receipt (55%) and Bangladeshi men the lowest (just 27%). For many of our respondents, the decision to claim 'sickness' benefits was not taken lightly, and the claiming process was stressful and time-consuming. Respondents across all four ethnic groups held concerns about the undesirability of claiming ill-health-related benefits, which were related to the perceived negative implications of assuming the identity of 'unfit for work' or 'disabled'. Such concerns were particularly strong among the Ghanaians. However, limited access to information and specialist support appeared to be more significant obstacles, and ones that were heightened for many of the minority ethnic individuals. Ethnically dominated social networks resulted in differential access to information and 'know-how'. Receiving Incapacity Benefit/Income Support does not, in and of itself, appear to exclude people from the labour market. However, some recipients felt outside 'mainstream' society and expressed strong preferences for (re)-entering the world of work. Nevertheless, some Incapacity Benefit/Income Support recipients had no plans to (re)-enter employment and were nevertheless leading productive and fulfilling lives.

Lack of social participation is both a dimension of poverty in and of itself and may also undermine access to other important resources. Most respondents identified maintaining social contact and accessing social support as major concerns since the onset of ill health. Most minority ethnic respondents socialised primarily within their ethnic group, and the four groups showed some distinctive patterns in types of informal and formal social activity. Social relationships were often important in facilitating access to more formal types of support from the state or voluntary agencies. Bangladeshi and Pakistani networks carried particular reciprocal obligations. Bangladeshi, Pakistani and particularly Ghanaian women were more constrained in their social contact than White English women or men from their communities. Quantitative analyses suggested that such differences were only partly explained by low income. Quantitative analyses also indicated that for men caring was associated with lower social participation, but that ill health was not. For women, ill health was linked to lower social participation, but caring was not. However, qualitative analyses suggest that many individuals *experience* social participation less positively in the face of ill health, often because social ties do not provide valued support. Social networks were often a burden for Bangladeshi and Pakistani women with chronic ill health. A complex of factors makes securing social support from informal networks difficult including: reluctance to seek help; fear of using up favours; the need to reciprocate; mistrust; and feelings of vulnerability. Formal groups and organisations are often no better at providing valued practical and material assistance. Many individuals were reluctant to join ill-health-specific groups, particularly when the perceived focus on talking about ill health is not felt to be useful. Individuals with higher income appeared better able to maintain social participation and to secure the types of social support that they need. Black Africans (and Ghanaians in the qualitative work) had particularly high risks of social isolation.

The study findings highlight the need for the current UK welfare reform agenda to be accompanied by an equal stress on entitlement and supporting people in fully claiming benefits for which they are eligible and which will at least partially ease some of the stresses associated with chronic ill health. Intervention aimed at increasing awareness, overcoming aversions to claiming and providing specialist support is particularly needed. There is also a need to increase the appropriateness of assessments of 'fitness for work'. Current approaches fail to recognise employability as a contingent and dynamic process, dependent not only on the condition, but also on the other characteristics/skills of the potential employee and the labour market options available. The continuing use of capacity for (any) work as a yardstick for assessing benefit entitlement is overly narrow, potentially stigmatising and unfair to those who, much as they would like work, fail to get it. For those with long-term health conditions, insufficient consideration to their experiences of pain, fatigue and the burden of hospital appointments may make fitness-for-work assessments unreasonable.

Although employment remains a core part of identity to many with long-term ill health, these perceptions vary with stage of life and with the type of work that can be carried out or is anticipated. Job search support and help with the transition to employment must be appropriately targeted and consider the full range of options, without falling back on stereotyping assumptions. An approach to job search and job training that links holistically to social support provision and carers' assessments is recommended. Furthermore, more attention must be given to the quality of employment that is on offer and the likelihood of job retention, since 'poor' work can exacerbate health conditions and is unlikely to be sustainable. There should also be more recognition of the multiple obstacles to employment faced by many individuals with long-term conditions and support for alternative positive 'outcomes', such as voluntary work, where appropriate and desired. Our study findings therefore illustrate the need for the welfare reform agenda to address the question of potential inability of those deemed 'capable' of work to actually find a job (or a stable job), and consider what levels of support might be appropriate in such circumstances – rather than assuming the current overwhelmingly punitive stance.

The policy focus on engaging employers and instituting appropriate workplace practices to support those with long-term conditions before they become economically inactive is welcome. However, the tension between employers' needs for a reliable workforce and the unpredictable and disruptive nature of much long-term ill health requires careful consideration. At present, many individuals with long-term health conditions are reluctant to reveal their ill health and to claim their right to employment.

There is also a need for increased recognition that ill health affects whole families rather than 'simply' the individual, and that competing priorities exist. In particular, households often combine both dependent children and adults with a chronic health condition. In such cases, work may not be regarded by those with multiple caring roles as the most appropriate way of maintaining the welfare of family members. Employment policies need to be sensitive to the differences in configurations of households, and, when engaging with aims for abolishing child poverty, adequately consider how the overall welfare of children, including older children, is best maintained.

In terms of support to individuals and families in managing and positively adapting to long-term health conditions, it is clear that much needs to be done. Few of our respondents were receiving any kind of 'formal' support to positively adapt to living with a long-term condition and many felt isolated, unsupported and lacking control over their lives. Furthermore, for many respondents, concerns about financial insecurity and hardship, immigration issues, or family disputes, overshadowed ill-health-related symptoms, and support services must therefore recognise the complex realities of people's daily lives and offer support in a holistic fashion. It is clear that group-based provision will not suit everyone and there is a need for diverse modes of support to those living with long-term ill health. Particular attention must be given to supporting those who have long-term mental health conditions.

The particular sets of circumstances that characterise the experiences of those belonging to certain ethnic groups, and the tendency for individuals to regard seeking support and services on the basis of shared ethnic identity as meaningful, suggest that the provision of interventions in ethnically specific ways is appropriate. However, diversity within and between groups must be recognised, so that the relevance of ethnicity, if any, for particular outcomes can be clearly understood. Furthermore, it is clearly important to meet the needs of minority ethnic individuals without furthering their marginalisation and isolation from 'mainstream' services and opportunities, something that was keenly felt by many participants.

Background and methodology

SUMMARY POINTS

- Long-term health conditions affect a large proportion of working-age adults in the UK, often limiting daily activities, employment chances and incomes.
- This heavy burden of long-term ill health is now of major policy concern across the UK health and social welfare arenas.
- Government interventions aim to increase self-reliance among those with long-term ill health and reduce the costs to the state of such conditions.
- However, protecting individuals and families who experience long-term ill health against poverty is currently less subject to direct attention.
- Research has highlighted the association between long-term ill health and the risk of poverty, and the far-reaching effects that such health conditions can have on individuals and their families.
- Less is known about the pathways that link ill health to poverty or how they may be broken. In particular, little attention has been given to social participation, access to non-labour income, and other knock-on effects.
- In Germany and the US the consequences of long-term ill health appear to be worse among minority ethnic groups, but little is understood about why this should be so, and these issues have not been examined in any detail for the UK.
- The present study integrates secondary analysis of national quantitative datasets with new in-depth qualitative data to explore the links between long-term ill health and dimensions of poverty.
- The study investigates: the ways in which family, community and wider society affect responses to long-term ill health (Chapter 2); the ways in which individuals adapt to having a long-term condition (Chapter 3); and the links between long-term ill health and employment (Chapter 4), access to welfare benefits (Chapter 5) and social participation (Chapter 6).
- The relevance of ethnicity is explored, although not assumed, across each of these areas, with a focus on four diverse ethnic 'groups': Pakistanis, Bangladeshis, Ghanaians and White English.
- Implications for policy and practice are discussed in Chapter 7.

Background to the study and research aims

Over the last century significant changes in demographic and disease profiles have resulted in ageing populations and a rising prevalence of long-term health conditions across Western Europe. Improved medical care and treatment mean that large numbers of people now live long lives with illnesses that were once thought of as killers; including heart disease and cancer. At the same time, there has been an increase in other long-term conditions, particularly mental illness and those related to lifestyle factors, including diabetes. Labour Force Survey data for September 2004, revealed that around 27% of working-age adults had a long-term health problem with 16% regarding it as activity limiting.[1] This heavy burden of long-term ill health is now of major policy concern across the health and social welfare arenas in the UK. The 2006 Welfare Reform Green Paper *A new deal for welfare: Empowering people to work* devoted specific attention to 'helping ill or disabled people'. This paper announced changes to the rules and procedures for receipt of sickness benefits[2] as well as new initiatives aimed at increasing the numbers of people who remain in, or re-enter, employment despite long-term health conditions (DWP, 2006a). At the same time, the UK public health agenda places increasing emphasis on patient choice and individual responsibility for health and the need to reduce the burden of long-term care to the NHS; priorities are laid out specifically in the Public Health White Paper *Choosing health: Making healthy choices easier* (DH, 2004a) and the White Paper *Our health, our care, our say: A new direction for community services* (DH, 2006).[3]

Current government interventions, particularly the expansion in lay-led self-management programmes (or the Expert Patient Programme)[4] and welfare-to-work initiatives (such as the Pathways to Work pilot for Incapacity Benefit recipients[5]), aim to achieve increased self-reliance among those with long-term health conditions and at the same time reduce the costs of such conditions to the state. However, other ways in which individuals and families experiencing long-term health conditions might be protected against (or lifted out of) poverty are currently receiving less attention. It can be argued that the current policy emphasis on paid work 'as a defining characteristic of citizenship or as the major route out of social exclusion' (Craig, 2004, p 98) gives insufficient attention to (a) the need for security for those who cannot work, (b) the fact that many forms of employment offer good returns neither in terms of pay nor in terms of participation in society, and (c) the fact that there may be other forms of participation that are more valuable and relevant for some individuals.

Recent research has drawn attention to the way in which long-term health conditions may contribute to the risks of poverty. An analysis of poverty dynamics using the British Household Panel Survey indicated that 8% of cases where an individual moves into poverty are triggered by a rise in the number of household members with limiting illness

---

[1] UK national surveys have employed a range of similar, although not identical, questions to ascertain levels of long-term health conditions. The terms 'long-term', 'chronic' and 'longstanding' are commonly used interchangeably in the UK research and policy literature, and only in some circumstances is a time period explicitly stated. These terms indicating an enduring nature are variously combined with 'health condition', 'health problem', 'illness', 'illness or disability' and 'illness, impairment or disability'. In addition, questions about the extent to which conditions limit day-to-day activities are also often used to gain a measure of 'limiting long-term illness', although again there is variation in the exact measures used in different surveys and studies. In the present study we opt to use the terms 'long-term health condition' and 'long-term ill health' interchangeably to refer to illnesses and impairments that have an onset during adult life and are ongoing without the prospect of a cure. We describe our operational approach below.

[2] See Chapter 5 for details of sickness benefits available in the UK in 2006.

[3] The present project also has relevance for the Department for Work and Pension's Public Service Agreement target on minority ethnic groups' employment, and the related work of the (cross-departmental) Ethnic Minority Employment Task Force; the carers' agenda, specifically the 2004 Carers (Equal Opportunities) Act; and the disability rights agenda and the 1995 and 2005 Disability Discrimination Acts, as discussed in Chapter 7.

[4] In 1999 the Expert Patients Task Force was set up to design a programme for people with long-term health conditions that would support people to increase their confidence, improve their quality of life and better manage their condition. It is the central plank of the Department of Health's agenda for increasing the capacity of patients to 'self-care' (DH, 2005).

[5] Pathways to Work was introduced in October 2003 as a pilot package of measures aimed at increasing the number of Incapacity Benefit recipients who move into paid work. The scheme has been gradually expanded and is planned to be delivered by private and voluntary sector providers as well as Jobcentre Plus so that by April 2008 it should be available to all Incapacity Benefit claimants.

and 16% by a rise in the number with poor mental health (Jenkins and Rigg, 2001). Child poverty is particularly affected by adult limiting illness (Adelman et al, 2003), and recovery from ill health is also identified as an important route out of poverty (Jenkins and Rigg, 2001). Other recent analyses of dynamics have highlighted the complexity and diversity of relationships between income, employment and ill health (Burchardt, 2000a; 2000b). However, little is known about the pathways that link ill health to poverty or how they may be broken. The coping strategies[6] used by individuals and households living with long-term health conditions and the ways in which these might be supported in order to buffer against a decline in living standards, or offer an escape from poverty, are also poorly understood.

Evidence from the UK and other settings suggests that the impact of long-term health conditions on individuals and their families may be diverse and far-reaching. Both care-giving and the extra costs associated with long-term illness and impairment have been investigated (Baldwin, 1985; Martin and White, 1987; Matthews and Truscott, 1990; Berthoud et al, 1993; Ahmad, 2000; Zaidi and Burchardt, 2004; Young et al, 2006). However, less attention has been given to other issues including social participation, access to non-labour income, and other types of knock-on effects for household members.

While there is evidence from Germany and the US that the consequences of long-term health conditions are not uniform across population subgroups, with higher risks of negative outcomes among minority ethnic groups (Arrow, 1996; Bound et al, 2003), little is understood about why this should be so, and these issues have received relatively little attention in the UK.

The research objectives of the present study were, then:

- To describe the relationships between long-term health conditions in working-age adults and indicators of well-being, poverty and social exclusion of individuals and households.
- To document the range of social, economic and cultural resources that individuals and households draw on in responding to long-term health conditions.
- To identify routes via which individuals and households experiencing long-term health conditions can be better supported in order to protect and improve living conditions and well-being.

The study also aimed to explore whether and in what way ethnicity was relevant to each of these domains.

Conceptualising poverty, long-term ill health and ethnicity

The broad project aim was to inform policy and programme responses to the growing numbers of individuals experiencing long-term health conditions (and associated impairment) in adult life. Although we acknowledge Ahmad's (2000) observation that the distinction between 'disability and chronic illness' (p 4) is often blurred in reality, the academic literature and policy discourses relating to these two areas often remain distinct. We therefore draw primarily on the large body of work that seeks to understand from

---

[6]   In the caring and long-term illness literature, a lack of conceptual clarity has been noted, with the term 'coping' being used to refer both to the ways in which individuals and families deal with difficult situations and the outcome of these efforts, that is, how successful they are (Nolan et al, 1996). We prefer to consider 'coping' as the strategies and activities pursued in response to stress or difficulty, and this is consistent with much of the literature on poverty and social exclusion.

patients' points of view what it means to live with a long-term health condition, much of which has explored particular illnesses (such as diabetes).

Although the emphasis of this work has undergone a number of shifts (Lawton, 2003; Bury et al, 2005), a common theme has been to recognise that the experience of long-term ill health is not merely medical, but rather social. Medical models of illness and disability focus on the impairment or condition as the 'problem' and direct intervention towards this dimension. In contrast, social models highlight the ways in which society responds to illness and impairment, often rendering them disabling. (See further the discussions in Braddock and Parish, 2001, and Swain et al, 2004.)

Negotiations and social interactions, particularly with family members and care-givers, are central to the experience of living with a long-term condition (Charmaz, 2000). Much of this work has been preoccupied with the degree to which individuals manage to positively adapt to living with long-term ill health and similar conditions have been shown to have diverse implications for different individuals (Bury et al, 2005). The implications of individual and family responses to long-term ill health for poverty and well-being have, however, received less attention.

Our approach to the present study was influenced by this body of literature in that we gave particular attention to examining (a) the role of people other than the individual with the long-term condition, (b) diversity in people's responses to ill health, including both negative and positive implications of the condition, (c) the significance of people's life stories and their ideas about who they are, and (d) the influence of wider community and societal factors beyond the family.

In relation to point (d) above, we were also influenced by so-called 'livelihoods approaches', which understand poverty to relate to more than just material resources and income. Instead, individuals and households are seen as actively managing complex sets of interrelated resources (Wood and Salway, 2000). Room (2000) suggests that households can be thought of as being endowed, to a greater or lesser extent, with 'resources', 'relationships' and 'welfare entitlements'. 'Resources' include not only material capital (current income, assets, stores, savings, gifts) but also 'human' capital (skills, education and, importantly, health status). 'Relationships' include networks within and beyond the household, links within the local neighbourhood, religious and ethnic communities, and also a person's relationship to the labour market. Relationships give individuals access to various resources, but these arrangements are informal and therefore may be unpredictable. 'Welfare entitlements' refer to the various types of support provided by public and private organisations, which are based on formal entitlements underpinned by state legislation. In the UK context, the tax and benefit system should play a major role in cushioning the effects of ill health. However, in practice access to benefits may be difficult, particularly for certain groups, and the amounts of benefits received may be inadequate to ensure a decent standard of living.

This way of thinking about the processes that create and perpetuate poverty led us to pay particular attention to the ways in which (a) social networks influenced, and were influenced by, access to material resources, (b) people prioritised different parts of their lives and held diverse opinions as to which 'outcomes' were most important, (c) individuals actively developed strategies for coping with long-term ill health and the extent to which these involved relationships within and beyond the household, and (d) wider societal factors (such as labour markets, housing markets, transport networks, education system, benefit system) provided opportunities to, or constraints on, individuals.

Finally, it is important to note that the relevance of ethnicity was considered, although not assumed, throughout our analyses. It is increasingly recognised that ethnic differentials in health outcomes, including the experiences and implications of long-term health conditions, must be understood not simply as the result of 'cultural differences' but rather within the context of wider social, historical, economic and political factors (Anderson et al, 1989; Ville et al, 1994; Higginbottom, 2006). In order to achieve this understanding, research must consider more critically what 'ethnicity' actually means (Smaje, 1996; Bradby, 2003; Karlsen and Nazroo, 2006). Conceptualising ethnicity in terms of *identity* is useful. Rather than thinking of ethnicity as something that is fixed and clear cut, much recent work has highlighted the ways in which ethnic identities may change over time and be multiple or hybrid (Gardner, 2002). At the same time, it is recognised that ethnic identities are defined from the outside as well as within and that there are limits to the ways in which individuals can fashion their own identities (Ville and Guerin-Pace, 2005). Importantly, holding a racialised identity remains central to the experience of minority ethnic individuals in the UK (Modood, 1988, 1998; Jenkins, 1994; Karlsen, 2004). In addition, family and the wider ethnic community may constrain individual identities both directly through the use of sanctions (as when parents punish children for behaving in 'culturally' inappropriate ways) and indirectly via the loss of social networks and the resources they may bring.

Drawing on these newer ways of thinking about ethnicity, we sought to understand first, why and how people identify themselves and others as inside or outside of particular ethnic groups in particular contexts; and second, the implications of such inclusion and exclusion for (a) the attitudes, preferences and behaviours ('ways of being and doing') that individuals adopt, and (b) their access to or exclusion from resources (broadly defined). Such an approach reminds us of the need to look closely at what is implied by ethnic identity in particular situations and to explore diversity *within* ethnic groups as well as similarities across groups.

Methods

The project employed a mixed-methods approach in which the collection of new qualitative data was combined with quantitative analysis of existing national survey data.

Qualitative

In our qualitative work we wanted to explore the links between long-term health conditions and poverty within and across a set of ethnic groups with diverse health and socioeconomic profiles. It was decided that four contrasting ethnic groups, namely Bangladeshi, Pakistani, Ghanaian and White English, would provide adequate opportunity for comparative analysis. A geographically focused approach was taken, both because this was logistically easier, and also because the location of residence was likely to be of relevance to understanding experiences of long-term ill health (Chapter 2). The qualitative work was therefore largely conducted in the East London boroughs of Hackney, Tower Hamlets and Newham, although some data collection also took place in Haringey, Lambeth and Southwark for Ghanaians. While appreciating that the content and boundaries of ethnic group membership are not fixed, in practice the research team identified potential respondents for the four 'groups' of interest and then sought to understand what ethnic identities meant to individual respondents as part of the research process. This approach proved relatively unproblematic for the Bangladeshi and Pakistani individuals, who, by and large, strongly identified with these ethnic labels, and for whom there were many ethnically based community organisations that served as points of contact. Locating Ghanaian respondents was more difficult. Although the notion of a Ghanaian 'community' was felt to be meaningful to many of our respondents, it was found to be much less visible and more geographically dispersed and there were fewer organisations and activities that were overtly Ghanaian, although churches proved useful. Interestingly, 'outsiders', such as professionals working in the area, were also less able to refer suitable respondents, with individuals of diverse African heritage being sent in our direction. Finally, seeking out suitable White English respondents proved time-consuming. Individuals themselves did not readily self-identify on the basis of ethnicity, there were no community organisations that were overtly for White English people, and professionals working in the area were uncomfortable with the fact that our work was seeking to single out this group (see McLean and Campbell, 2003, for similar research experiences).

Three phases of qualitative data collection were conducted during our fieldwork period, which lasted from March 2005 to May 2006. First, a phase of 'rapid assessment' was carried out by the research team and a group of trained community researchers. A geographical 'community' was identified for each of the four ethnic groups through consultation, and a series of informal conversations, mapping/ranking exercises, key informant interviews, group discussions, ethnographic interviews and observations were then employed (see Appendix A). The aim of this phase was to gain a broad overview of the patterns of social, economic and cultural resources available to members of the four communities as well as an understanding of how long-term ill health is perceived and the prominence it has in people's everyday lives. This phase also informed interview guideline development and the identification of suitable participants for Phase Two.

In Phase Two, in-depth interviews were conducted with (a) working-age adults with a long-term health condition and (b) individuals living with someone who had a long-term health condition, usually an adult child or spouse.

Although in practice many long-term health conditions bring impairment we nevertheless explicitly avoided using the term 'disabled'. The intention was to include a broad range of conditions (rather than to restrict the sample to those who self-identified as 'disabled'). A requirement of our sample was that the health condition should be ongoing and onset should have been during adult life. In practice, our fieldwork took a very open-ended, flexible approach, although clearly identification of potential respondents required us to use some terms to indicate who we were looking for. We tended to use the terms 'long-term health problem', 'long-term health condition' and 'long-term illness' (and their equivalents in local languages where available).[7] On occasion, we also offered examples of conditions that might be considered as 'long term', although no precise definitions of degree of severity, duration or interference with daily activities were employed. This approach allowed us to explore subjective interpretations of ill health and its consequences, as well as the extent to which individuals adopted a 'disabled' self-identity (see Chapter 3).

A total of 86 detailed interviews were available for analysis: 57 of these were interviews with individuals with a long-term health condition (47 completed in Phase Two and 10 completed in Phase One), and 29 were interviews with family members. Overall, 22 interviews were completed with Bangladeshis, 20 with White English, 22 with Pakistanis and 22 with Ghanaians. We ensured that our respondents were mixed with respect to health condition, age, sex, migration and employment characteristics. However, our intentional focus on East London communities meant that our respondents were, by and large, from more deprived socioeconomic groups. Respondents reported a very wide range of health conditions. The majority had conditions that were primarily associated with a

---

[7] Among Bengali/Sylheti speakers the term '*chirourughi*' was often used as the appropriate translation, although the term literally means 'permanent illness'. Among the Urdu/Punjabi speakers we found no equivalent term but instead used the expression '*lambe arse ki bimari*', that is, 'illness of long duration'.

long-term illness,[8] the most common of which were heart disease, diabetes, depression and arthritis, although there were some who had suffered accidental injury. Many respondents reported more than one condition and experienced pain, fatigue and unpredictability of symptoms as core elements of their health condition. The characteristics, including all the health conditions that were reported, for our interview respondents are presented in Appendix A. It should be remembered that we gathered information from many more people than were interviewed in depth through the use of additional data collection methods in Phases One and Three.

Interviews, while being open ended and flexible, included history-taking methods to explore individual and household trajectories over time. Interviews were conducted in the language of respondent's choice by members of the research team and, subject to respondent approval, were tape-recorded and transcribed. The research team included fluent speakers of Bengali, Sylheti, Urdu, Punjabi, Hindi, Twi and Ga. Over half of the interviews with Pakistanis and Bangladeshis were conducted in languages other than English, although among the Ghanaians only two respondents chose not to be interviewed in English. In a small number of interviews it was felt that the respondent had chosen English but would have been better able to express themselves in another language. Translations into English were carried out by research team members and other experienced translators with whom we were in close contact. The focus was on retaining conceptual consistency (Atkin and Chattoo, 2006) and in many cases we opted for the transliteration of significant words and phrases so as not to lose meaning.

Analysis and interpretation of findings were ongoing during data collection. Researchers kept field diaries and held regular meetings and analysis workshops in which emerging findings and ideas were shared. Part-way through the second phase of data collection the information gathered was reviewed and some adjustments were made to the data collection tool to ensure that further detail could be gathered on issues of interest. A coding scheme was developed for use with the software package Nvivo through an iterative (three-stage) process involving line-by-line blind coding of a subsample of transcripts by three qualitative researchers. Once finalised, the coding structure was applied to the interview transcripts and, through multiple 'search-and-retrieve' actions, information from across the range of respondents was brought together for further theme building. This 'code and compile' approach was complemented by detailed memo writing for each respondent using a consistent guideline in which themes running through each story, contextual information and more interpretive comments (for instance regarding inconsistency between the individual with long-term ill health's reports and those of the other family member, or obvious omissions) were noted.

Finally, a phase of 'community feedback and consultation' was undertaken during which emerging findings were shared via a series of five informal meetings. This allowed study participants and other community members to consider the validity and usefulness of study findings, and to comment on the ways in which they represent their community. Detailed field notes were taken and the salient points integrated with earlier findings. The findings presented in the chapters that follow draw on evidence generated during all three phases of data collection, although quotations from the second phase interviews with individuals with a long-term health condition and family members are most commonly used to illustrate the points being made.

---

[8] We use the term 'illness' to refer to respondents' own perceptions of having abnormal bodily functioning. In fact, most respondents also reported medical diagnosis of one or more particular 'diseases', where a disease can be defined as the pathological condition of a part, organ or system of the body or mind resulting from various causes, such as infection, genetic defect or environmental stress, and characterised by an identifiable group of signs or symptoms.

Quantitative

Three quantitative datasets were used. First, we used the Labour Force Survey (LFS), a nationally representative survey covering around 60,000 individual respondents each quarter. We used this survey to examine the relationship between long-term ill health and (a) labour market status and (b) use of benefits. The LFS is a semi-panel survey in which each respondent is surveyed at five consecutive quarters. We pooled multiple quarters to ensure sufficient numbers of minority ethnic respondents: 12 quarters from 2002-05 for analysis of benefit use and labour market position and 16 quarters (using wave 1 responses only) from 2001-05 for analysis of pay. We used the question: 'Do you have any health problems or disabilities that you expect will last for more than a year?' We exploited the panel element of the survey to remove some of the 'noise' associated with the health questions by requiring that, to be counted as having a long-term health condition, the respondent had to have answered positively to the question in the subsequent quarter as well as the current one. Thus, we effectively excluded all wave 5 responses and included an additional quarter of data for the construction of this variable. We also made use of the question (addressed to those who had already positively answered the first question): 'Do these health problems or disabilities, when taken singly or together, substantially limit your ability to carry out normal day to day activities?' We refer to those who responded positively to this latter question (and who were already included in our long-term health condition measure) as those with 'an activity-limiting health condition'. In addition, we used number of conditions reported to approximate severity of ill health.

We used the Office for National Statistics (ONS) question on ethnic group to carry out analysis for the four groups that corresponded most closely to our qualitative sample, that is Bangladeshi, Pakistani, Black African and White British (see also discussion on pages 9-10 on integrating approaches). We employed descriptive statistics for the topics of interest and binary and multinomial logistic regression models (as appropriate). The regression models allowed us to investigate whether apparent ethnic differences could be explained by differences in other characteristics relevant to our outcome variables. Moreover, we specifically explored whether there was any evidence for ethnic differences in the associations between long-term ill health and employment (see Chapter 4).

Second, we used the household file of the LFS (HLFS) to investigate the structure and composition of households containing working-age individuals with long-term ill health. The household file covers approximately 55,000 households at each quarter and is available for the spring and autumn quarters of each year. We pooled six quarters from 2002-04 to ensure sufficient numbers for analysis, resulting in around 334,000 cases, representing 190,000 unique households. We used this household dataset to describe patterns of employment and caring in households with a member with a long-term health condition. We used the ONS question on the ethnic group of the household reference person to explore variation in these associations by ethnicity.

Third, we used the 2001 Home Office Citizenship Survey (HOCS)[9] to investigate the relationships between long-term health conditions and social participation. The HOCS is a biennial cross-sectional survey designed to capture ethnic differences in citizenship and community experiences. It is specifically employed to monitor aspects of inclusion and community cohesion in relation to the UK's reporting responsibilities under the European Union Lisbon goals. It includes a booster sample of 5,000 members of minority ethnic groups as well as the 10,000-person main sample. This survey included the question: 'Do you have any long-term illness, health problem or disability which limits your daily activities or the work you can do?', which we used to identify individuals with a limiting

---

[9] We had some unresolved questions about the quality of the ethnicity data for 2003, so we therefore used the 2001 sweep instead.

long-term health condition. In addition, we examined outcomes for individuals who reported 'regular caring responsibilities' for someone within the household or elsewhere. Patterns of social participation were explored by ethnic group (again using the ONS categories), health status and caring status, using descriptive statistics and ordered probit regression models (see Chapter 6).

Throughout the elaboration of the quantitative analysis, we focus on discussion of the results. In particular, we summarise results of regression models rather than supplying tables of coefficients, which are not always straightforward to interpret. We focus on discussion of results that are statistically significant at the 5% level (and in the LFS analysis this is having adjusted standard errors for repeat observations on individuals). We also employ graphical illustrations of relevant results, including predicted probabilities from the regression models, where it clarifies the argument. Full regression tables for all the analyses are available from the authors.

Integrating approaches

The above description of methods has indicated a number of ways in which the samples for the qualitative and quantitative components of the study differed. Our qualitative work can be considered to have generated data relating to a subset of the sample included in the quantitative datasets for three reasons.

First, the way in which individuals were categorised as having a 'long-term health condition' differed slightly between the datasets. Our qualitative work was designed specifically to inform policy and programme responses to the growing numbers of individuals experiencing long-term health conditions (and associated impairment) in adult life and we therefore intentionally excluded individuals who had had health conditions since birth or childhood, and also avoided using the term 'disabled' during recruitment of participants. However, our quantitative work utilised existing datasets, which, as noted above, grouped together individuals reporting 'health problems or disabilities that you expect will last for more than a year' in the case of the LFS, and 'long-term illness, health problem or disability' in the case of the HOCS. Clearly, then, these survey data will include individuals who have been experiencing their health condition since childhood. It is also likely that the survey data include some individuals who regard themselves as having a 'disability' but not a 'health problem', 'health condition' or 'illness'; individuals who would not have been included in our qualitative work. Clearly, the distinction between 'disability' and 'long-term illness' is not clear cut and it is unlikely that the different definitions employed by the qualitative and quantitative approaches compromise their compatibility. We therefore opt to use the terms 'long-term health condition' and 'long-term ill health' interchangeably to encompass the range of conditions that were included in the study.

The second area of difference between our data sources relates to geographical spread. Whereas the LFS and HOCS data derive from a national sample, the qualitative work took place primarily in East London. Exploration of Census data indicates that levels of long-term ill health were higher and socioeconomic conditions poorer in our study areas than nationally (see Chapter 2). However, since the objective of the research project was to explore the links between long-term health conditions and various dimensions of poverty, such a geographical and socioeconomic focus was warranted.

Third, it is important to consider the differences in the ways in which ethnic group membership was operationalised in the two approaches and in the ethnic categories available for analysis. As noted above, our qualitative work focused on four contrasting ethnic 'groups', namely Bangladeshi, Pakistani, Ghanaian and White English and allowed us to examine the extent to which such categories were meaningful and the implications they had for individuals' lives. In contrast, our quantitative analyses were restricted to using the ONS question on ethnic group, and there was less scope for exploring the relevance of these categories. We concentrated on the four groups that mapped most closely onto those in our qualitative sample: Bangladeshi, White British, Pakistani and Black African. Clearly Black African is a much more heterogeneous category than our Ghanaian sample (itself containing different linguistic and ethnic 'groups'). However, it is likely to include the vast majority of those who define themselves as Ghanaian and it is the closest approximation we could arrive at to our Ghanaian sample. The White British category is also somewhat broader than our White English sample, but the disparity is much smaller. It will include most of those who define themselves as White English, who numerically dominate the category, but it will also include White Scottish, White Welsh and some White Irish.

Notwithstanding these differences, the integration of qualitative and quantitative methods provided a much more comprehensive investigation of the links between long-term ill health and poverty across diverse ethnic groups than either one approach would have provided. The qualitative and quantitative approaches were considered to be complementary (Adamson, 2005), allowing us both to explore in detail the ways in which individuals and families experience and respond to long-term ill health and also to describe the aggregate levels and differentials in access to key resources: employment, welfare benefits and social participation. The research team included individuals with both qualitative and quantitative skills and the two pieces of work were guided by a common set of theoretical assumptions and research objectives. During the course of the project the qualitative and quantitative work proceeded side by side with regular feedback of emerging findings between the two. The writing-up process was also conducted in an integrated fashion with particular team members taking responsibility for considering the qualitative and quantitative evidence on particular topics and bringing the two together to provide an integrated account.

Overview of the report

We start our discussion of the study's findings in Chapter 2, by setting out the ways in which family, community and society structure the resources that individuals with long-term health conditions and their family members can draw upon in responding to ill health. In Chapter 3, we present findings relating to ways in which individuals adapt to living with long-term ill health. These two chapters form the backdrop for the subsequent three chapters – 4, 5 and 6 – which look at the implications of long-term ill health for three key areas that impact upon individual and household poverty: employment, welfare benefits and social participation. Chapter 7 considers the relevance of the study's findings to policy and practice across the health and social welfare arenas.

2

Family, community and society: placing long-term health conditions in context

SUMMARY POINTS

- The immediate family is the primary resource for managing the impact of long-term ill health.
- Ethnic groups vary considerably in household composition, with important implications for the completion of tasks, including caring.
- Family members are often constrained in their ability to shift roles in response to ill health. Caring for children alongside an adult with long-term ill health can make paid work very difficult.
- Levels of long-term ill health differ significantly between ethnic groups.
- 'Community' membership affects the impact of long-term ill health, via both the social networks it confers and the resources available locally.
- Social relationships are often important in facilitating access to more formal types of support from the state or voluntary agencies.
- For the minority ethnic respondents, membership of an 'ethnic community' was meaningful and brought access to opportunities and support, but also expectations, obligations and constraints.
- Although experiences of direct racist discrimination were rarely reported, general feelings of exclusion from 'mainstream' White society and services were widespread among minority ethnic respondents.
- Recent policy emphases and wider public opinion can affect the way individuals feel about themselves and their condition, as well as their entitlements from the state.

Introduction

Family, community and wider society influence the social and economic consequences of long-term health conditions in complex ways. Family and household structure, particularly the absence of potential adult workers and presence of dependent children, have been shown to exacerbate the impact of long-term conditions (Parker, 1993; Drewett et al, 1994; Mutchler et al, 1999). Existing literature has also described the importance of the family as a resource in managing the impact of ill health. In the short term, the family is the first reserve for dealing with symptoms and diagnosis (Bury, 1991). In the longer term, the practical limitations brought on by the health condition often imply a transformation of family roles and relationships. Prior research has emphasised that the capacity to 'weather' these problems depends on the pre-existing quality of family life and the personalities of the individuals involved (Parker, 1993). Some families do break down, more commonly soon after onset rather than after a long period of strain (Locker, 1983). At the community level, there has been some interest in informal community care and the involvement of friends, neighbours and acquaintances beyond the family (see, for example, Drewett et al, 1994). However, the implications of belonging to a particular community, such as access to resources and expected patterns of behaviour, have been given less attention. Furthermore, the wider social climate impacts upon individuals, and this should also be examined. Here we draw on both qualitative and quantitative data to describe some of the processes and pathways through which family, community and society appear to influence the experiences of living with a long-term health condition among our four ethnic 'groups' of focus: Bangladeshis, Pakistanis, White English and Ghanaians (or Black Africans in the quantitative analyses).

Family and household

Important commonalities were found across the four ethnic groups in the impact of long-term health conditions on the family. Furthermore, within each ethnic group, there was a lot of variation in the ease with which families made adaptations. However, family size, structure and the ways in which family roles are organised varied to some extent across the ethnic groups, and these differences had implications for the ways that families responded.

Family members, care and support

The family members who were at hand within the household varied substantially. Restricting our analysis to households containing at least one person of working age with a long-term health condition, Table 1 illustrates the differing composition of households across the ethnic groups. Among the Black African group, almost a quarter were single-person households – that is, by definition, people living on their own with a long-term condition – and thus with no potential co-resident carers or alternative workers.

Table 1 also shows the very high proportion of lone-parent households among Black African households. In these households, the demands on the lone parent will be substantial: not only caring for dependent children but also attending to their own health (or, in some cases, that of a non-dependent child); as was the case for a number of our respondents in the qualitative work. Conversely, non-dependent and even

Table 1: Household composition by ethnic group: households containing one or more people of working age with a long-term health condition (% of households)

	White British	Pakistani	Bangladeshi	Black African
Single person	17.4	6.3	3.3	24.4
Couple without children	28.7	6.9	3.5	7.8
Couple with dependent children	25.7	47.3	51.6	21.0
Couple with non-dependent children only	10.6	5.6	4.4	1.5
Lone parents with dependent children	7.1	9.9	11.2	27.4
Lone parents with non-dependent children only	4.2	2.3	2.2	4.6
Complex (multiple-family) households	6.1	21.7	24.1	13.3

Notes: 'Complex households' include multiple-family households (including where the 'family' consists of a single person), and couple or lone-parent families where people other than (dependent and non-dependent) children are present. Same-sex couples have been excluded due to the very small proportions, particularly from the minority groups. Ethnic group is attributed to the household on the basis of the ethnicity of the household reference person. *Source:* HLFS 2002-04, authors' analysis dependent children may be providing care and support to their parent or taking on the role of caring for younger children. By contrast, the high number of complex (multiple-family) households among Pakistanis and Bangladeshis (22% and 24% respectively) may maximise the possibility of available carers or those able to take on alternative roles that the individual with a long-term condition can no longer manage (although it may of course imply other problems, particularly overcrowded living conditions). Around 50% of Bangladeshi and Pakistani households with a long-term ill member consisted of couples with dependent children, compared with just 26% of the White British group, among whom couples living alone were the most likely household composition (29%). These household-level data can, of course, tell us nothing about the extent to which there are family members living close by, who provide important care and support, a pattern that was commonly revealed in the qualitative work.

Despite important diversity in household composition, our qualitative work indicated strong areas of commonality between the ethnic groups in the involvement of family members in care and support. First, it was evident that support is frequently a source of tension across all the ethnic groups. In common with other work (for example Katbamna et al, 2000) our findings dispel the stereotype of cohesive 'South Asian' families with unproblematic support structures.

Second, there were also strong commonalities in the types of kin who the respondents felt they could turn to in practice for support and care, most commonly spouses/partners and adult children. Similarly, across all four groups, daughters were more likely to be drawn into supportive roles than sons. The respondents also held common understandings about the desirability of children being sheltered from the impact of ill health.

Most respondents had contact with family living outside the household, including relatives in other cities and other countries in the case of our minority respondents, and received various forms of support from them. Childcare provided by local grandparents was particularly valued in freeing up parents to do other work. However, members of the extended family did not generally become involved in the everyday management of the health condition (such as maintaining medication regimes or dietary requirements) and its knock-on effects (such as increased household maintenance work). There was often a gap between the expectations people held and the provision of support from relatives beyond the household, particularly among the Pakistanis and Bangladeshis who commonly felt that certain family members were obligated (culturally and religiously) to provide certain kinds of support. In all groups, the provision of support rested critically on the strength of affection between specific family members, although this was most pronounced among the White English respondents. The feeling that children today failed to respect and support their parents was common – 'traditional' expectations about family caring were in a state of flux and being replaced with an individualism in which people 'had their own lives' or 'did what they liked'.

Respondents' stories revealed variation in the extent to which families engaged in collective planning, managing and sharing of income and other resources. Although variation within the ethnic groups should not be ignored, collective activity was most evident among the Pakistanis and Bangladeshis, often extending across the members of multiple households, and usually involving individuals related through the male line (although this was not absent among the other groups). For instance, purchasing of houses, educational fees and trips 'back home' would all commonly be funded through arrangements among multiple adult members of an extended family. In contrast, although some White English respondents referred to relatives as sources of financial support and advice in times of need, the management of family resources and the long-term well-being of family members were the concern and responsibility of the nuclear family, primarily the husband–wife couple. Among our Ghanaian respondents, within the nuclear family, separate money management by spouses/partners was found to be common, with women and men directing their income to different expenditures, particularly their own parents and siblings who remained in Ghana with whom some degree of sharing of resources was common. Clearly, such differential patterns of income sharing have implications for the resources over which family members with long-term health conditions might have a legitimate claim, and the individuals who can be called upon in times of need.

Adaptations to family roles and responsibilities

In all families, individuals other than the person with the long-term health condition have a stake in how the condition and its knock-on effects (for instance withdrawal from paid employment) are managed. The extent to which family members adjust their roles depends on perceived options and their desirability; factors that are in turn dependent on a range of external factors such as the local labour market, and socially expected behaviour, as well as personal preferences. In general, we found much evidence of inflexibility surrounding the roles that individuals played in families.

The effect of an individual's health condition on the likelihood of another family member adjusting their pattern of employment was varied. Some family members, particularly spouses, but also adult children, had to take time off work to provide direct care or, more commonly, to take on childcare or be a companion for medical appointments. The latter was a particular issue for Bangladeshis and Pakistanis who often lacked the necessary English language skills and confidence to negotiate the health service alone and there was greater expectation that individuals would be accompanied than among the White English or Ghanaians. Taking time off work for the health needs of another family member was very difficult and had led in some cases to leaving employment completely.

> 'They used to call me to work ... they need me, but I had personal problem at home. So before I try the sick note, you know, they don't accept. Then I go for without pay leave for three months. After that I left the job [in 1992].' (Bangladeshi man, family member, 55-59 years)

In other cases, family members had altered their working patterns to accommodate the needs associated with the health condition, for instance by working part time, taking work closer to home, or taking a night shift, and thereby managed to remain in employment.

However, in some cases across all the ethnic groups it appeared that individuals prioritised their income-earning role and made few allowances for the health condition of the family member. This was particularly true of men (although not absent among women) and seemed often to relate to a combination of refusing to recognise their wife's health condition, a reluctance to take up a caring or home-maker role and the importance given to their self-identity as income-earner.

The departure from employment of the main family income-earner due to ill health is not necessarily a trigger for others to start work; in fact it can have quite the opposite effect. In some cases, caring requirements limited the potential employability of 'alternative workers' following the onset of the breadwinner's condition, although it was clear that perceptions of need and demand for care varied greatly. Caring often took a toll on particular individuals, usually women, who could even feel exploited. Many of our Bangladeshi and Pakistani female respondents referred to social pressures to be seen to be caring appropriately for their husbands with long-term conditions, making the uptake of a working role more difficult and a lower priority.

In cases where the health condition had become 'all-consuming' because of its severity and/or the emotional response to it (see Chapter 3), family members felt overwhelmed with day-to-day household tasks and taking up employment had not even been considered.

> 'No, I am busy with children, looking after children. Now, I'm busy with my husband and children. How could I work? He's ill and so…. Because he is my husband I have to look after him. I can't just leave him behind and go away anywhere. I have to be with him all the time.' (Bangladeshi woman, family member, 30-34 years)

The value attached to family maintenance also tended to restrict flexibility in household roles, particularly among the minority ethnic groups, for whom cooking food from 'back home' was an important and morally loaded symbol of cultural belonging and of women correctly fulfilling their expected female roles.

There was some evidence that family roles were more flexible among the Ghanaians than in the other communities, with caring and productive roles less clearly opposed to one another, particularly for women. Furthermore, the high prevalence of lone-parent households clearly precluded the division of types of work between men and women in many cases. However, across all four groups there was more evidence of women assuming income-generating roles than of men picking up household tasks. Nevertheless, women across all four groups gave their mothering (and grandmothering) roles high priority and in a number of cases sought to emphasise these when long-term health conditions compromised their ability to perform paid employment. Furthermore, when husbands or partners experienced health conditions, women were not always willing to sacrifice their childcare role and go out to work.

> 'I've still be really wanting to stay at home and look after my children. Obviously I could have just said right he's not working I need to go and get a job and have my children looked after. But I really didn't want to. So I basically had to put up with just been living on benefits which obviously isn't very much money…. So I just feel that I … my children get a good quality of life from actually having a lot of time with us but then maybe they don't have like the holidays abroad or the latest toys and things.' (White English woman, family member, 40-44 years)

Furthermore, in some cases the health condition was such that husbands were unable to adequately perform household work or childcare, further limiting the possibility of role-switching between spouses. Negative social attitudes towards men performing household work (evident to a greater or lesser extent across all the communities, but particularly marked in some Pakistani, Bangladeshi and Ghanaian families) further restricted the flexibility of household roles.

Notwithstanding these commonalities across the communities, there was evidence among some of the Pakistani and Bangladeshi households (although by no means all) that men with long-term conditions were reluctant for their wives to work because it was seen as further undermining their role as head and provider for the household. Some Pakistani and Bangladeshi women in turn actively clung onto their responsibility for household work and childcare, regardless of their husband's health, often reflecting their limited alternative sources of recognition and status within the family.

Furthermore, quantitative analyses showed significant variation between the ethnic groups at the aggregate level in the extent to which childcare and caring roles exist alongside each other, which may make substitution of roles, and taking up employment more complicated, as our respondents indicated. Seventy-nine per cent of Bangladeshi households containing a working-age adult with a long-term health condition also contained a dependent child, compared with 66% of Pakistani households, 49% of Black African households and just 30% of White British households.

Moreover, if we consider caring and employment as potentially competing with each other, we see that the likelihood of there being 'potential carers' in a household (defined as working-age adults who do not have a long-term health condition and are not working) also varied substantially by ethnic group (Table 2); from 13% of White British households to 64% of Bangladeshi households. Moreover, the presence of 'available carers' may be particularly important in households with children, both to provide care for them and to protect them from taking on caring roles themselves (although such responsibilities are not necessarily experienced negatively). Again, a much higher proportion of Bangladeshi and Pakistani households (at 66% and 60%) had such 'available carers' than Black African or White British households (at 35% and 19%). This difference partly reflects ethnic differences in family composition; but the qualitative findings discussed above suggest that different approaches to prioritising caring versus breadwinning, a reluctance to relinquish childcare roles, the perceived demands of caring, as well as the perceived unavailability and low rewards of employment, may discourage people from being economically active.

Long-term health conditions are also not evenly distributed across households. Instead, particular households may have several members with long-term conditions while other households are free from ill health. Examining those households with at least one working-age adult with a long-term condition, analysis of the HLFS showed that 44% of Bangladeshi households in fact contained two or more people (including older people) with such a condition, compared with 39% of Pakistani households, 28% of White British households and 15% of Black African households. Although these ethnic differentials again in part reflect the differing household structures, nevertheless, the co-existence of several health conditions within one household is likely to create added strain and further restrict the ability of household members to adapt. Our qualitative work included several families with more than one member experiencing long-term ill health. In such cases, caring and supporting between these family members was often complex and reciprocal.

Clearly, complex caring demands co-exist in some households meaning that family members' interests may not necessarily be best served by adults/parents (with and without long-term health conditions) being in paid work, particularly when the economic returns to such work are not high (see Chapter 4); a point not lost on many of our respondents.

Table 2: Availability of 'potential carers': households containing one or more people of working age with a long-term health condition (% of households)

| | | | Households with 'potential carers' | |
	None	Yes, all working	Yes, all not working	Yes, some not working
White British	44.8	41.7	8.5	4.9
Pakistani	24.5	23.5	29.2	22.8
Bangladeshi	19.9	15.8	39.5	24.9
Black African	53.4	18.3	20.7	7.6

Source: HLFS 2004-06, authors' analysis

Multiple household stresses and financial hardship

Long-term health conditions are often just one of many stresses that individuals and family members have to deal with. Our respondents often talked about their health condition as inherently connected to other problems in their lives including marital instability, family conflict or domestic violence, worklessness or financial insecurity. In addition, many of our minority ethnic respondents faced problems related to their country of origin and, for some, their status as migrants. For Bangladeshis and Pakistanis, transnational difficulties commonly related to the need to financially support elderly relatives 'back home', the high costs of international travel and health conditions making such travel impossible. For several more recent Ghanaian migrants, their immediate families were split between Ghana and the UK, causing much distress and meaning limited networks of support locally. Long-term health conditions complicate and in turn are complicated by these other problems, so that stresses begin to reinforce one another and may make managing extremely difficult.

Across all four ethnic groups, the link between long-term health conditions and financial hardship was a prominent one. A decline in earnings was the most common reason for this link. However, respondents also spoke of the increased expenditures associated with long-term health conditions, particularly in relation to special dietary needs and the added costs associated with impaired mobility. Respondents described not only having to go without and needing to budget carefully, but also the mental stress that living on a low income brings. Many respondents spoke of savings being exhausted and accumulating debt. As one key informant in Phase One noted: 'People feel overwhelmed by debt, they don't open their letters, bills'. Respondents found not being able to afford things for their children particularly upsetting. Financial hardship was also reported to lead to family tension and conflict by many respondents, although some individuals did seem to find it easier than others to come to terms with their limited resources.

> 'Before I just used to buy it and not have to worry. Not like I'd have a great big wage packet and lots of money, but just to be able to, you know, not always have to think about it all the time. Not to have to work it out – if you spend money on that then you're not going to be able to do all these things.' (White English woman, family member, 40-44 years)

Respondents whose only income was welfare benefits often felt particularly vulnerable, and many respondents reported getting into financial difficulties due to benefits being delayed, stopped or reduced without warning.

Families were found to adopt various strategies not only to reduce expenditure but also to make keeping track of bills and expenses easier and less stressful. Nevertheless, it was apparent that over the long term, living on a low income had significant implications for quality of life as things wear out and break down and homes fall into disrepair. Costs of transport seemed to be a particular issue for many with long-term conditions. Giving up a car to reduce expenditure had left some housebound. Buses were often inconvenient and difficult to manage, while taxis were prohibitively expensive.

Although these issues affected individuals across all the ethnic groups, the Ghanaians stood out as being most at risk of financial hardship because of their often weak support from scattered family members and their lack of entitlement to welfare benefit (due to recent migration) and generally poor knowledge of the system. In contrast, it was evident that several of our Bangladeshi and Pakistani individuals with long-term health conditions were financially supported by their adult children, although this clearly depended upon life-cycle stage and was not true across the board. The White English experience of financial support within families was mixed and highly dependent upon the closeness of particular relationships. Several of our White English respondents were entirely dependent on benefit income, although some who had worked in the past had occupational pensions and savings as added buffers against financial hardship.

Community

Membership of a community has relevance for the experiences of individuals living with long-term health conditions and their families in two related ways: first, via resources held at the community level, which may be drawn upon; and second, via the options and constraints placed on individuals by community norms and expectations.

Meanings of community: ethnicity and location

The majority of respondents felt that it made sense to speak of a community in their local area and most expressed a sense of belonging to such a community. However, the ways in which ideas about community related to location and ethnicity were complex and context specific.

For the Ghanaians, Pakistanis and Bangladeshis it was clear that ethnicity (understood primarily as a shared country of origin and common 'culture') was a salient part of self-identity (that is, the way people felt about themselves) and that their ethnicity implied being part of an 'ethnic community'. Despite evidence of diverse lifestyles within these communities (particularly according to socioeconomic status and generation), respondents nevertheless talked about shared ethnicity bringing a sense of 'feeling easy' or having a common 'understanding'. Importantly also, shared ethnicity entailed expectations and informal claims to support, advice, information and advocacy (although such claims were frequently compromised by health conditions, as discussed in Chapter 6). In our Pakistani and Bangladeshi fieldwork areas, dense patterns of settlement meant that daily interactions predominantly involved other individuals from the same ethnic group. Furthermore, family networks, including links to Bangladesh or Pakistan, remained active for many, binding the members of these communities together both socially and economically.

The Pakistanis and Bangladeshis were particularly reliant on intra-ethnic contacts for work and support, including support with negotiating state agencies. A reliance on inclusion in informal networks opens up possibilities and accesses certain resources, but also entails exclusion from others, and a narrowing of what is known and possible.

> 'I used to feel very scared and fearful going up to the doctors ... I had nobody to support me.... My parents were there but they are old and don't speak English. I had no Bengali person who could support me ... I had nobody to guide me or let me know that I had other options.' (Bangladeshi woman with long-term condition, 35-39 years)

Having noted the significance of being 'Ghanaian', 'Pakistani' or 'Bangladeshi', it is important to recognise that subdivisions were evident within these 'groups', and that these divisions had some implications both for the types of behaviour and attitudes that people adopted and, importantly, the networks of resources and support that were open to individuals. Such subdivisions were most evident among the Ghanaians, reflecting the diverse linguistic, cultural, religious and socioeconomic profile of this 'group'.

A strong sense of belonging to a particular ethnic community was frequently combined with feelings of alienation from 'mainstream' White society and its facilities. Although our minority ethnic respondents did not often talk about racism in the form of active exclusion, the fear of racism could be a powerful deterrent to the take-up of services and opportunities. Furthermore, many minority ethnic respondents recounted the extreme difficulties they had faced in accessing services and support from varied government agencies. Although similar problems were also mentioned by White English respondents, such experiences seemed to exacerbate minority ethnic respondents' feelings of exclusion and further encouraged reliance on 'our own people'.

'How can I explain it to you? If you was to go somewhere there's just all White people there's all this people, you will look at yourself twice and think 'In there? No!' Do you know what I mean? But, you just feel funny. Yourself, you would just feel funny going in there.... I don't really hear or see people saying things to me. It's just the way you feel. That you don't see yourself in there, full stop.' (Ghanaian family member, 20-24 years)

Among the White English respondents, ethnic identity was experienced less in terms of a shared identity based on similarity, and more as a marker of difference from others. Many White English respondents had reservations about 'losing their culture' because of the influx of minority ethnic people into their locality, and saw White ethnicity as an impediment to accessing resources that they saw as earmarked for other communities. Among the White English respondents there were many links with the Black Caribbean community – mixed marriage, for example, was not stigmatised – but nevertheless social networks tended not to be ethnically diverse. However, shared ethnicity was not used in the same way as by minority ethnic individuals to reach beyond personal social relationships to access information and support.

The socioeconomic profile of an ethnic community clearly influences the resources that are on offer to its members. Current social and economic circumstances of UK minority groups in turn relate to their histories of migration and settlement (see Ballard, 1996; Peach, 1996; Modood et al, 1997). The generally limited education and marketable skills possessed by the early Pakistani and Bangladeshi migrants, originating mainly from the remote and underdeveloped regions of rural Azad Kashmir and Sylhet, differ strikingly from the first wave of Ghanaian migrants, who were often highly educated and purposively recruited for skilled work. Early occupational concentration in manufacturing and heavy industry has had an enduring impact on the socioeconomic security of Pakistanis and Bangladeshis in an era of deindustrialisation. Furthermore, the persistent concentration within a narrow range of occupational sectors restricted the options open to these groups when responding to the demands of long-term ill health. Despite these similarities, differences in cultural heritage, mother tongue and migration circumstances between Bangladeshis and Pakistanis should be recognised (Haskey, 1997) as well as the more extreme indicators of deprivation among Bangladeshis (Platt, 2002). In our qualitative study areas, the distinctiveness of these two communities was readily apparent with obvious residential segregation, independent development of community resources, and distinct employment patterns. Bangladeshi men were heavily concentrated within the restaurant sector and few Bangladeshi women were working. Pakistani men had a more diverse profile of manufacturing and service sector jobs and Pakistani women had often done paid work at some time during their lives. In contrast to these two groups, the Ghanaian community appeared to have a much more diverse profile in terms of employment types and socioeconomic circumstances, potentially offering more avenues to opportunities.

In addition to ethnicity, location was a significant dimension of community for many respondents, reflecting the fact that people with long-term health conditions and low income tend to spend much of their time close to home. Nevertheless, the extent to which ideas of community were bound up with location varied. For many of the White English respondents, their sense of community was closely tied to place. Both the Pakistanis and Bangladeshis also had a strong sense of their local area, and also local history, in part defining their community. As with the White English, this geographical community did, at times, include those outside their ethnic group. However, it was also clear that a great deal of energy had been (and continues to be) expended in constructing an ethnic community in these areas, as evidenced by the large numbers of community organisations, mosques, language schools, services and shops serving the needs of community members. Eade (1997) has described how the entry of second generation Bangladeshis into the political and administrative arenas of Tower Hamlets in the 1980s and 1990s has influenced public discourse regarding the needs and rights of the Bangladeshi community. There was less infrastructure specifically catering to the Pakistani community in Newham than to the Bangladeshi community in Tower Hamlets. However, Pakistani involvement in the council and voluntary sector in Newham has placed the needs and rights of Asians and Muslims on the political agenda. Importantly too, however, the 'community' for these groups did at times also span other geographical areas with high concentrations of the same ethnic group. For the Ghanaian respondents, their community seemed less linked to a particular geographical location, and often appeared to cover several locations within London, which had residential concentrations of Ghanaians and key resources such as community centres and churches. There was much less evidence of active construction of a Ghanaian community concentrated in a particular area, and where we did come across coordinated community activity it related more to development projects in Ghana than to the UK setting.

Nevertheless, where people lived was important, providing a backdrop of resources that may be drawn upon in response to long-term health conditions: council policies, the housing stock, transport links, local services and voluntary/community organisations can present opportunities and obstacles for individuals and families. Having relatives living nearby may make help more easily accessible on a day-to-day basis for households affected by long-term ill health. However, the extent to which families can live close together and provide such support is constrained by local authority rules and conditions in the housing market. White English respondents described how their families had been dispersed by local authority policies regarding the allocation of council properties, with resultant lack of support in times of need (see also Dench et al, 2006). Several Bangladeshi families remained in overcrowded conditions because suitable council housing could not be allocated to them within the area and they were unwilling to move away from much-needed family support networks.

Long-term health conditions at community level

The extent to which a community carries a high burden of health conditions is also an important contextual factor in understanding how individuals respond to their own ill health. Pervasive ill health will impact upon the resources that can be mobilised from the community and may also shape attitudes. Drawing on tables from the 2001 Census, levels of long-term ill health[10] among people of working age in our qualitative study areas (Tower Hamlets, Newham and Hackney) were found to be substantially higher than those for England and Wales as a whole, at around 10% compared with 8%. Similarly, we find that the percentage who considered themselves to be in 'not good health' (a measure that asks people to rate themselves relative to those of the same age) is around 1 percentage point higher in the study areas.

Drawing on national LFS data, Figures 1 and 2 show the proportion of men and women reporting a long-term health condition and the proportion reporting a long-term health condition that limits daily activities, broken down by ethnic group. Beyond age 30 the levels reported start to diverge between the groups: Bangladeshi and Pakistani men and

---

[10] In the 2001 Census the question was: 'Do you have any long-term illness, health problem or disability which limits your daily activities or the work you can do?'.

Figure 1: Proportions reporting a long-term health condition by ethnic group

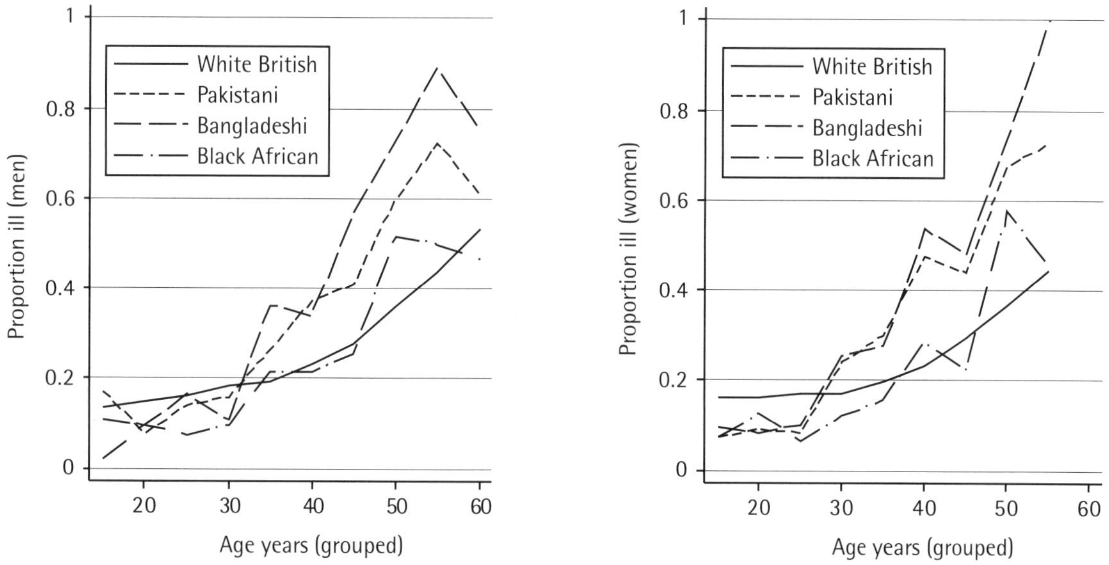

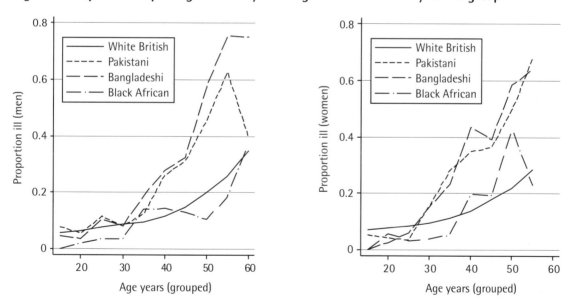

Notes: Age-specific proportions use person weights. The measurement of long-term health condition is constrained by requiring a 'yes' in both the following as well as the current quarter (see Chapter 1). Proportions have been estimated across five-year age bands. 'ill' is shorthand for having a long-term health condition.
Source: LFS 2002-05 (pooled quarters)

Figure 2: Proportions reporting an activity-limiting health condition by ethnic group

Notes: Age-specific proportions use person weights. The measurement of long-term health condition is constrained by requiring a 'yes' in both the following as well as the current quarter (see Chapter 1). Proportions have been estimated across five-year age bands. 'ill' in this figure is shorthand for having an activity-limiting health condition.
Source: LFS 2002-05 (pooled quarters)

women were much more likely to report health conditions than the White British or Black African individuals at ages beyond 40. This pattern is broadly in line with that shown in the 2001 Census data, although the definition of long-term health condition differs slightly between the two data sources (see Appendix B).

Interestingly, we found these differing aggregate levels of ill health among the ethnic groups to be reflected in community-level awareness of long-term conditions. Many

Pakistanis and Bangladeshis perceived certain conditions to be extremely common in their communities, talking about diabetes and heart disease in particular and referring to the 'Asian diet', lack of exercise, lack of knowledge and stress as key causes. Among the White English respondents, long-term ill health was often felt to be related to the ageing and 'dying out' of the White English community, with talk about strains and exhaustion due to hard physical work and mental illness due to social problems. Among the Ghanaian respondents there seemed to be an incipient awareness of long-term conditions, particularly hypertension and related premature death. These were explained in relation to an intense Ghanaian 'work ethic', leading people to work too hard and 'burn themselves out'. These different community-level understandings were found to have implications for individual-level responses to long-term health conditions, as well as access to information and services (themes taken up in Chapters 3 and 5).

Social and cultural expectations of behaviour: pressures from community

Belonging to an ethnic community carried expectations and pressures regarding appropriate behaviour, which opened up certain possibilities for action and constrained others. Many Pakistani and Bangladeshi respondents felt the 'moral community' (*mashra* in Urdu and *shomaj* in Bengali) as a pervasive presence in their lives. The moral community is associated with 'proper living': morally laden ways of behaving that are felt to be distinctly Pakistani or Bengali, and often defined in opposition to a perceived 'English' culture. Most of the Ghanaian respondents held similar ideas, although the morally significant ways of life were less tied up in notions of sexual propriety and the behaviour of women. For many minority ethnic respondents, the 'community' emerged as a somewhat oppressive presence in their lives, monitoring and judging behaviour, while at the same time being the main potential source of support. Interestingly, some of the White English respondents did also worry about 'what others would think or say', but this was a much less salient part of everyday decision making.

Religion was a further important dimension of belonging to a community for many Pakistanis, Bangladeshis and Ghanaians; providing additional justification for expected behaviours, avenues to social contact and emotional sustenance.

Society and state

Many of our respondents' lives were closely entwined with state bureaucracy, with individuals commonly being involved in applications, negotiations and disputes with multiple agencies (for instance the benefit system, housing authorities, social services, the National Health Service [NHS] and, for the minority ethnic individuals, the immigration authorities). Recent developments in government policy relating to health and social welfare seemed to have a tangible, often negative, impact on respondents' experiences of health and social services. Many (although not all) respondents felt that the quality of healthcare received was inadequate and a result of changes in government policy. Difficulties making appointments and a feeling that health providers did not have time to listen and address the patient's needs were common.

> 'He didn't seem too interested, you know, he was like basically more interested in giving me pills and telling me to bugger off.' (White English woman with long-term condition, 20-24 years)

Likewise, many of the respondents who had experience of sickness certification and claiming sickness benefits felt that their claims had been rejected due to state drives to reduce the number of claimants (see Chapter 5). Awareness of such government policy shifts, and the associated media and public questioning of the entitlements of those with long-term health conditions, appeared to contribute to feelings of illegitimacy and worthlessness (see Chapter 3). No discernible ethnic differentials in these issues were apparent.

Many respondents across the groups felt insecure about their claims to support from the state, although these issues tended to be more common among the minority ethnic groups. For recent migrants, immigration status was often a source of considerable worry. We encountered a wide range of situations – some respondents had entered the country on work permits or as spouses and had no entitlement to welfare benefits, some had overstayed, and some were currently legally resident but their past illegality (such as using a false National Insurance number or working cash in hand) made them feel insecure about exercising their rights. Concerns about immigration status meant that some individuals were wary of engaging with any statutory services, including general practitioners (GPs). For new migrants with limited social support networks, having a long-term health condition tended to complicate matters — plans to work were thwarted, the option of returning 'home' was no longer attractive (since there would be no access to free healthcare), and new support needs often could not be readily met. More generally, poor English language skills and unfamiliarity with the system made negotiating formal entitlements difficult for some.

State provision rests on assumptions about how families should function that were sometimes at odds with the realities of respondents' lives. For instance, the assumption and requirement that resources are pooled between spouses/partners was felt to be unfair by some of the respondents. For means-tested benefits, if one partner's earnings tipped the couple over the income threshold for the benefit then the other partner was not eligible to claim, which meant that they were entitled to less than if they had been single. Moreover, in practice not all spouses/partners shared their income with one another and many respondents wanted to have a benefit income that was clearly designated as their own.

The low levels of financial support given to informal carers was felt to express the assumption that caring is an axiomatic part of certain family members' roles. Moreover, the few respondents who had investigated claiming Carer's Allowance had found the system to be complex and inflexible, leaving them unrecognised and unrecompensed.

Furthermore, the principle of independence that guides the provision of state support to those with long-term health conditions and disabilities may also be at odds with the realities of respondents' lives. Many respondents *did* want to be independent, but the type of support that was given to facilitate this was not always appropriate. For example, a wheelchair-bound Pakistani respondent was given council housing in a White English neighbourhood, but chose instead to stay living with her cousin because she felt she needed the support of her relatives and community living nearby.

The feeling that the 'system' was unfair and inappropriate was expressed by respondents across the four ethnic groups. However, these experiences could be heightened for the minority ethnic respondents, many of whom felt alienated and excluded from 'mainstream' society in other ways. Some of the Pakistani, Bangladeshi and Ghanaian respondents harboured specific concerns about the ways in which state provision clashed with what they saw as their 'culture' or failed to take account of the experience of being part of a minority ethnic group. For example, a Ghanaian respondent felt that her 'traditional' role as grandmother had been undermined by social services who failed to include her in consultations about the appropriate course of action when her daughter's health was felt to be compromising the well-being of her grandchild.

Conclusions

Family, community and wider society provide the resources that individuals and family members draw upon to manage the problems raised by long-term health conditions, and as such shape the processes through which long-term conditions and poverty are linked. The formal entitlements and informal claims to these resources, however, are shown to be complex and deeply interrelated. Claiming formal entitlements can be dependent on the strength of personal relationships, as for example when the capacity to use job agencies to find work depends on securing childcare from family members outside the home. Some people are more heavily dependent on relationships and informal claims than others, as for women whose resources are often concentrated in the family, or migrants whose formal entitlements may be lacking. Furthermore, the heavy reliance on support from people within one's own ethnic community, as was evident for Pakistanis, Bangladeshis and to a lesser extent Ghanaians, can mean that access to formal entitlements is dependent on informal relationships and therefore becomes less reliable.

3

Individual experiences of long-term ill health: barriers and supports to 'resilience'

SUMMARY POINTS

- Developing 'resilience' (positive adaptation) in the face of ill health involves both mental adjustments (finding meaning in life and self-worth) and gaining control (coping strategies and experience).
- While some respondents showed remarkable buoyancy and enthusiasm for life, others were struggling and showed signs of serious emotional upset.
- Pressures to be 'normal' and hide ill health existed across all four ethnic groups, with negative implications for seeking healthcare and support.
- While holding onto prior roles and activities was a positive thing for some, for others it led to frustration and unhappiness.
- Achieving self-worth was particularly difficult for younger people with long-term conditions. Pakistani and Bangladeshi women also often struggled to feel valued.
- Close association with health services discouraged a sense of control for many via: long delays to diagnosis/treatment; lack of information and understanding; unpredictable symptoms; and frequent appointments.
- Family factors affected the development of resilience. Communication and consistency between the individual's perspective and those of other family members was important for their actions to be felt supportive.
- Few respondents received any support from external sources to developing any of the dimensions of resilience explored.
- Resilience (or positive adaptation) clearly takes a variety of forms and there was no one 'outcome' that was desirable for all.

Introduction

Investigations into the experiences of individuals living with long-term ill health have been numerous (see Charmaz, 2000; Lawton, 2003; and Bury et al, 2005, for useful reviews). Two consistent findings emerge. First, individuals do not, in general, passively consign themselves to 'being sick' but rather actively engage in a range of activities to manage their lives in the face of difficulty. Second, people's responses to long-term ill health are extremely varied, although many appear to successfully adapt, incorporating their health condition into their personal history (Williams, 1984), or even reinventing themselves in more positive ways (Charmaz, 2000).

Importantly, much of this work has drawn attention to the significance of how individuals think and feel about themselves (their identity) and their health condition. In addition, however, more recent work emphasises the importance of individuals developing concrete strategies for managing their situation, and gaining understanding and competence in coping over time, if they are to positively adapt, or gain 'resilience'.

In addition, there is increasing recognition that the resiliency process (or positive adaptation) will imply different types of 'outcomes' for different individuals. In particular, the assumption that striving to function in the ways one did before the onset of ill health (including maintaining one's prior occupation) is necessarily an indicator of positive adaptation has been challenged (Ville, 2005; Sharpe and Curran, 2006). Certain responses to long-term ill health can be 'double-edged', perhaps allowing individuals to accept their condition and stop dwelling on their symptoms, but at the expense of necessary treatment, care and support (Campbell et al, 2003; Bury et al, 2005, p 8). How such tensions arise and the implications they have for the ways in which individuals prioritise conflicting actions deserves further investigation.

Despite evidence of many commonalities across ethnic groups, particularly in the ways in which symptoms are reported (Njobvu et al, 1999, Nazroo and O'Connor, 2002; Hussain and Cochrane, 2004), there may be important ways in which ethnicity shapes the individual experiences. A number of studies of South Asians suggest that the degree of stigma attached to ill health (and impairment) and the way in which individuals are subject to monitoring by the family and wider community is more intense than among the White majority, resulting in a greater desire for concealment (Katbamna et al, 2000; Molloy et al, 2003). Although far fewer studies have included UK Africans, Molloy et al (2003) reported heightened stigma and concealment among their respondents of African origin. These factors may make it harder for individuals from some minority ethnic groups to develop resilience, although this has not been examined in any detail.

Relatively little is known about how individuals living with long-term health conditions can best be supported in developing resilience. Nevertheless, the above discussion would certainly suggest the need for pluralistic approaches. However, available evidence has tended to highlight the proscriptive nature of input that is offered across a range of interventions that are intended to be supportive (Anderson et al, 1989; Ville, 2005; Bury et al, 2005; Sharpe and Curran, 2006). In a variety of contexts, it has been noted that professional intervention may take control away from individuals and families and thereby fail to support the resiliency process. Support interventions may serve minority ethnic groups particularly badly. Several studies suggest that minority ethnic individuals with long-term conditions have a higher propensity towards self-care or 'management' of the condition within the family than the majority White population (Katbamna et al, 2000; Higginbottom, 2006). This in part reflects language barriers; but dissonance between individuals' and health professionals' interpretations of the condition and appropriate management strategies, and a consequent lack of trust and satisfaction with available services, are also factors (Anderson et al, 1989; Mirza and Sheridan, 2003; Higginbottom, 2006). Such patterns also imply the failure of government and voluntary agencies to fulfil their responsibility to make services accessible and appropriate to the needs of marginalised groups (Atkin and Rollings, 1996; Chattoo and Ahmad, 2003).

The above discussion suggests that complex and ongoing interactions between individuals and their surroundings determine the diverse ways in which long-term health conditions are experienced. Little is understood about what encourages resilience (positive adaptation) of individuals. Furthermore, the implications of different ways of responding to long-term ill health for other dimensions of well-being and poverty (including access to benefits, employment and social participation) have been little explored.

The present chapter draws exclusively on our qualitative work. We use the three interrelated dimensions of 'resilience' suggested by Grant et al (2007: forthcoming), to describe the ways in which individuals respond to long-term ill health, and explore how the process of developing 'resilience' may be constrained or supported. These dimensions are:

- adjusting to the situation and finding meaning in life
- achieving feelings of self-worth (a valued self-identity) and
- gaining a sense of control

Not unexpectedly, our qualitative fieldwork revealed great diversity in the individual experience of long-term ill health. While some respondents showed remarkable buoyancy and enthusiasm for life, others were experiencing their ill health as a constant struggle and showed signs of serious emotional upset (indeed several had clinical diagnoses of depression and some reported having had suicidal thoughts). The actual nature of the condition played an important part in these diverse experiences. The extent to which individuals experienced pain and disruption to their daily lives varied greatly, as did the degree to which their condition was outwardly visible to others. However, it was also apparent that similar physical experiences (and impairments) meant different things to different people. Furthermore, it was clear that the experience of ill health was not determined by individuals in isolation, but rather other people, particularly family members (who often had a significant stake in the process), and professionals often played an important part.

Adjusting to the situation and finding meaning

As Charmaz (2000, p 275) states, 'experiencing serious illness challenges prior meanings, taken for granted ways of living, and ways of knowing self. Life is now uncertain. The self has become vulnerable and, thus, problematic'.

Whether and how individuals make mental adjustments to these challenges was found to vary greatly. In the words of a key informant from the Phase One fieldwork, 'some people go on kicking and screaming all the way, whereas others are able to accept the situation'. Some respondents were very aware of their own process of mental adjustment (or search for meaning) and described how this had been gradual, and in some cases was still ongoing.

> 'Well, I do miss going to the pub and that sort of thing, but you know I've accepted it now, you know, I can go but I just choose not to because I don't enjoy it, it's not the same as it used to be.... I've learnt to accept it, I think I've probably gone, what's the term? Like full circle, from like when I first was ill not being able to accept it, I found it hard to accept, but I've really accepted it now.' (White English woman with long-term condition, 40-44 years)

Furthermore, several respondents identified the ability to 'accept things the way they are' as part of their prior self-identity so that adjusting to ill health and 'getting on with it' were in themselves an affirmation of their prior self.

> 'I never did. I never [thought of myself as long-term ill]. I'm not a person to dwell on things at all. I'm not ... I don't think it's been hard but everybody around me thinks it's been hard. But I'm not a person to think like that.... You just get on with it.' (Bangladeshi woman with long-term condition, 25-29 years)

Family-level support emerged as important for many of the respondents who had made mental adjustments to their new situation.

'Initially when I first came out [of hospital] I was very, very, very despondent, and then, you know, I had good support from my sister and family and I gradually. My close, the people I would consider closest to me, they had accepted what had happened, at first I couldn't accept what had happened to me but then, you know, they started saying 'you know C we've got to realise that you are lucky to be here, 'cos some people don't get through it, or they lose an arm, a leg, whatever', and then I started to think 'well yeah you're right' and I started suddenly. Not overnight. I can't put a time on it. But suddenly started to think more positive about things and think well, yes I am lucky, your life's got to go on with or without [the health condition], your life's got to go on and you've just got to try and make the best of it ... you know?' (White English woman with long-term condition, 40-44 years)

However, many of our respondents had not managed to make the mental adjustments necessary to find meaning and fulfilment in life.

'Sometimes I think I haven't got a future, 'cause what do I do? I just sit here and stare out of the window and that ain't a future. You know, what's the future in that?' (White English man with long-term condition, 45-49 years)

Pressures to 'be normal' – concealing ill health

A factor that was particularly important to the experience of our working-age respondents, and one that may distinguish them from individuals who acquire illness or impairment earlier or later in life, was the reluctance to identify oneself as having a long-term health condition. While some respondents did assume an overt 'ill identity', many more resisted labelling themselves in this way. Furthermore, achieving positive mental adjustment to having the condition could be undermined by efforts to retain the illusion of 'being normal'.

Across all four ethnic groups concealing ill health and impairment was common. Concealment took a variety of forms including withholding information, taking care with physical appearance, using euphemisms or choosing a preferred label for the condition, attending social gatherings despite feeling unwell, refusing to use aids and direct lying. Despite this commonality, closer inspection revealed differences across the ethnic groups in the motivations and meanings attached to concealment, as well as the people involved.

White English respondents tended to talk about their downplaying of symptoms and concealment of the condition as a dimension of personal or, in a few cases, family character. In contrast, our minority ethnic respondents were more likely to explain their actions in terms of expected behaviour for their ethnic community; presenting concealment as an essential characteristic of 'our culture'. Among the Pakistani and Bangladeshi respondents, concealment was particularly associated with the feminine ideal of bearing distress in silence and gaining high moral status through suffering (the concept of being '*sabarwali*' in Urdu). Among the Ghanaians, concealment of health conditions was strongly identified as a typical trait for both men and women.

'I am not different, I am still Ghanaian, so I wouldn't particularly go about broadcasting my sickness you know.' (Ghanaian man with long-term condition, 50-54 years)

Furthermore, while respondents from all backgrounds expressed the desire for concealment in terms of individual pride and self-reliance, our minority ethnic respondents also commonly referred to the implications of the health condition for other family members, and concerns that information would spread quickly through the community, leading to gossip and negative behaviour. Concealment therefore reflected a perceived vulnerability and several respondents felt pressure from family and wider community to conceal their condition.

> 'I don't discuss my household problems with anyone. If you tell people, it's like you are naked [lifts up her kameez to emphasise the point]. Your secrets come out; you lose respect if you tell others about what is going on in your life.' (Pakistani woman with long-term condition, 40-45 years)

Of course, concealment occurred to varying degrees with some individuals not declaring their ill health outside the home at all, or even withholding information from family members. More often, ill health was revealed to a limited number of 'close friends' or trusted individuals, although efforts to downplay the extent of impairments and symptoms and appear 'normal' were still maintained.

> 'Yeah, they [relatives] do come down here sometimes, but I always put a brave face on it so people don't realise just how bad I am. Erm, but my mum has been like there since I've been diagnosed, but I don't think even she realises how bad it is because I do put a face on it and I try and put a smile on me all the time.' (White English woman with long-term condition, 20-24 years)

The extent to which a particular condition is thought to be abnormal is important. For all four ethnic groups, mental ill health was stigmatised and the desire to hide such conditions particularly strong. In contrast, diabetes and heart disease were familiar and considered relatively 'normal' among Pakistanis and Bangladeshis, resulting in a reduced need for concealment and easier mental adjustment to the idea of being someone living with these conditions (although some individuals still struggled). In contrast, among the Ghanaians, such acceptance was less common across the range of long-term conditions.

Clearly, the tendency to hide ill health can have negative implications and we found examples of individuals delaying seeking healthcare, not complying with treatment and not seeking, and even refusing, help or support.

> 'I had decided not to take any medication ... I told myself that I had to fight with life. I used to think in my mind that I have to live ... I have to make myself strong, not depend on medicines ... then I used five to six oils to massage and I felt better ... relaxed.' (Pakistani woman with long-term condition, 50-54 years)

Furthermore, such concealment was frequently at odds with the daily reminders of not being 'normal', particularly pain, fatigue, diet and medication regimes. While some respondents appeared able to balance an 'internal' recognition of ill health with 'external' concealment, more often this led to tension and unhappiness.

Importantly, there was particular resistance to accepting the label 'disabled'. In contrast to studies that have focused on individuals with severe impairments from early in life, we found few examples of individuals affirming a disabled identity. Respondents often sought to distance themselves from what they regarded as the unvarying and permanent nature of disability and its association with incapacity. Refusing to accept (or in some cases not even considering) a 'disabled' identity had implications for engagement with services that are identified in these terms, as discussed in Chapters 5 and 6.

'Social service people have registered me as a 'registered blind'. I couldn't accept this mentally. I used to say that I'm not blind. I used to think that if they consider me to be a blind person they would stop my treatment and would not see me. And give up. But then the doctor told me that it is not that they would give up. Instead this would help me in getting the services. Then I agreed. But I used to feel very unusual when I used to think that I am a registered blind. I could never accept this. I used to hate this term.' (Pakistani woman with long-term condition, 45-49 years)

Giving up or redefining roles

For many respondents, maintaining pre-existing roles and behaviours was an important part of the need to carry on 'as normal'. The threat of having to give up valued roles was often keenly felt, particularly because many respondents were aware that their health condition was likely to deteriorate over time. Such resistance was found in relation to a range of activities and roles, although concerns about paid employment, parenting, household maintenance and socialising were prominent. Furthermore, while some respondents appeared to focus on one field of activity as their primary concern, others emphasised multiple roles and activities they wished to maintain.

'I find it hard people helping me, and if they're doing that they, they are taking that little bit of independence away from me. It's like a home help. My friends they said get a home help. But it's my independence they are taking away. I don't want to lose, or feel that I am disabled. I don't want to give in to being disabled.' (White English woman with long-term condition, 55-59 years)

Of course, for many, paid employment was not only a central part of who they were (their self-identity) but also their primary source of income, implying particular importance to maintaining this role (Chapter 4). However, the threat of role loss could be equally challenging for those who saw themselves as home-makers. Several Bangladeshi and Pakistani women made every effort to maintain their household duties, not wanting to abandon this role due to lack of alternatives and, for some, a feeling of vulnerability within the household.

Holding onto prior roles and activities was clearly a positive thing in some cases, enabling the individual to retain meaning and fulfilment in life despite their health condition.

'If at any point during that time [in hospital] somebody had said to me 'you can't go back to work' or 'you'll have to find another job' I would have been devastated.' (White English woman with long-term health condition, 40-44 years)

However, in other cases it was clear that it led to frustration and unhappiness and was a reflection of the individual and/or other family members not having adjusted to the reduced capacity and increased needs accompanying ill health.

[Talking about struggling to remain in work in the face of ill health] 'It was very tiring for me and I also needed some rest. That [working] made me tired and also affect on my heart as well. I thought it was easy, but no. If it's taking too much, that will make me sick. That's not good. I don't want to take any risk on my health.' (Pakistani woman with long-term condition, 35-39 years)

'They do know about it, but they just think 'Oh, she's a good woman, let's turn up'. Oh, they don't think oh, you know, six of us turn up, the poor woman has to cook and stuff, you know, they just say 'Oh, she's a good woman, she won't say anything, let's just turn up', knowing that I'm probably not feeling well, that, you know, my arm … you know, you have to cook. Well, there's a difference between my culture and your culture, my culture, if somebody turns up you have to feed 'em.' (Bangladeshi woman with long-term condition, 34-39 years)

Not all respondents clung onto their pre-existing situation. Some individuals were more flexible than others; more able to adapt to new ways of being and to find meaning in them. The extent to which social roles could be given up or changed without serious threat to an individual's sense of self also varied with cultural context, socioeconomic position and family circumstances (as discussed in further detail in Chapters 2 and 4).

[Talking about doing household work rather than being employed] 'That's not a complete role that's just a little bit, something you can do to try and even things up but you always feel that you're being taken care of.' (White English man with long-term condition, 40-44 years)

[Talking about spending more time with her granddaughter since stopping work] 'I have been looking after her since she was two weeks old every other weekend, and when she is on holiday from school I have her for a week, like the six weeks' holiday. Me and her have got a very strong bond … as she's getting older she is looking more like my son, she's his double…. My granddaughter is my life.' (White English woman with long-term condition, 55-59 years)

Other family members' perceptions of the needs and capabilities of the individual with long-term ill health can also be extremely influential. In some cases, family members had actively supported the individual to resist incapacity and in others encouraged the giving up of roles and restriction of activities. However, effects were often more subtle and unintentional. Family members took away roles by, for instance, no longer seeking the individual's advice or not asking them to do things. Several respondents, from across the four communities, expressed frustration at their independence being compromised by other family members' actions and attitudes. In this way individuals were less able to find meaning and fulfilment in their new situation.

'The doctor says that I need to keep trying to do things but he [husband] won't let me. I know they are only trying to help…. They have taken control.' (White English woman with long-term condition, 45-49 years)

However, it was clear that striking the right balance between, on the one hand, supporting an individual in their mental adjustment to reduced activity and, on the other hand, smothering the individual, was often hard.

Overall, there was great variation in the extent to which our respondents had made the necessary mental adjustments to allow meaning and fulfilment in life despite their long term health condition. In some cases, the health condition still had relatively minor implications for the individual's needs and activities, and little such adjustment was currently demanded. However, in several cases, it appeared that respondents were putting off, avoiding (or simply unaware of) this important dimension. For instance, a White English woman had thrown herself enthusiastically into caring for her young baby, but was unable to think clearly about what her recent withdrawal from paid work due to ill health would mean in the longer term, and she was clearly scared by the prospect that her condition might be lifelong.

Achieving feelings of self-worth

Closely related to mental adjustment to changed circumstances is the need for individuals with long-term health conditions to achieve feelings of self-worth; something that many respondents found a constant struggle.

> 'I don't know the words to say. I feel lost. I'm fed up of being ill all the time ... I just don't feel good about myself. I mean things are not going good in my life and sometimes I think I can't take it anymore.... I feel as if I can't do nothing.' (White woman with long-term health condition, 45-49 years)

For many respondents, loss or perceived poor performance of valued social roles seriously undermined their feelings of self-worth. While for others the loss of vitality more generally clashed with their sense of who they were: 'I'm an active person and I can't be active no more. I get really, really angry about it. I really, really do' (White male with long-term condition, 45-49 years).

In contrast, feelings of self-worth could be boosted where new goals were identified and achieved, in several cases through voluntary work.

> 'I set up certain targets, like setting up the club and that sort of thing, um it's difficult to meet things really. I can help other people um if you do that. In a way I can give you a bit more time now [after ill health] than before. So you just try to set up things up.... [To a] lot of people, I can give information.... So in a way it's not been a waste. I can help other people, up to a point, which I can do.' (Pakistani man with long-term condition, 55-59 years)

Feelings of illegitimacy and guilt were common and were greater among younger than older respondents. Respondents in all four groups held similar ideas regarding the inevitability of increasing age leading to declining health and reduced activity. However, for Bangladeshi and Pakistani respondents this process related closely to life stage and the completion of life events (particularly marriage of children) so that the chronological age at which this was legitimately felt to happen was younger than for White respondents. For many Bangladeshis and Pakistanis in their forties and fifties, 'being in poor health' did not therefore appear to pose a serious conflict to their feelings of self-worth. Many men at this stage of life assumed the largely economically inactive role of 'elder' ('barhe' or 'morubi'), relatively easily (see Gardner, 2002), while women who had co-resident daughters-in-law could also withdraw from the central home-maker role. In contrast, for both male and female Ghanaian respondents age or life cycle in themselves did not appear to justify reduced activity and engagement in society, and so ill health had greater potential for undermining feelings of self-worth.

Recognition and acknowledgement from other people appeared central to the process of individuals (re)gaining a sense that they are valued and valuable. Feelings of illegitimacy and frustration were heightened for individuals whose other family members did not acknowledge the health condition, not only because support was denied, but also, importantly, because their integrity was questioned. Individuals with long-term mental ill health were particularly likely to face this difficult situation.

> 'It's taken her nearly four years to admit her daughter has got a mental health problem, you know, because she was like 'Oh there's no such thing as depression, you need to pull yourself together'. And I'm like 'Mum if it was that easy I'd do it. You know, I don't like waking up feeling like this. But I can't help it, it's not my fault, you know'. Erm, she has finally come to terms with it.' (White English woman with long-term condition, 20-24 years)

In addition to family members, health and welfare professionals can contribute to feelings of low self-worth, particularly where they call into question the individual's own perception of their health status. Many respondents reported feeling that their health condition was not taken seriously by their GP or other health professionals. However, some also felt that their sense of self-worth and confidence was undermined by health professionals portraying them as more seriously ill than they felt they were. Coherence between the individual's interpretation of their situation and that of other people seems to be important if their inputs are to be supportive. Reluctance to interact with the outside world for fear of stigma and negative reaction also undermined feelings of self-worth for some respondents.

> [Recounting the story of a failed appeal for Incapacity Benefit] 'I am not fit. I can't lift anything. I can't carry anything ... I explained everything to them, I am telling you in short cut but I explained everything. After five minutes they called me and said 'Unfortunately, after careful considerations, we can not help you out'. So I am out! I am not on sick benefit. To be honest, I am not cheating. I don't go to work. I am not lying or acting.' (Bangladeshi man with long-term condition, 35-39 years)

Religion emerged as important for many of the minority ethnic respondents, particularly the women. Both the routine afforded by regular acts of prayer and religious faith itself boosted feelings of self-worth in many of our Muslim and Christian respondents.

Gaining control

Among respondents who were struggling to positively adapt to their condition an important dimension was often feeling unable to take control of their situation: 'I just go lie on the bed and give up' (White English female with long-term condition, 45-49 years).

> 'When I'm ill I don't feel in control at all, you know, you feel so er so like you don't think you can get out of it. But as you gradually get stronger you feel you're taking things back into your own hands again. So at the moment I'm, I've made a lot of progress and I've probably still got a little way to go but I feel that things are in my hands now, that I can go forward a bit more.' (White English man with long-term condition, 45-49 years)

In contrast, several individuals appeared to have personal attributes of determination and positive thinking that helped them feel more in control of their situation. For instance, it was noticeable that some individuals yearned for a cure to their condition while others focused on managing their condition as effectively as they could with the medication and treatments available.

> 'Yeah, when I told them [the family] this is the case and this is what they [the doctors] told me to do and I'm going to see to it that I do that and that's all. And er ... I tried to calm them down as the head of the family, I tried to let people know what is happening. I am in control of it, so it shouldn't be a worry to anybody.' (Ghanaian man with long-term condition, 60-64 years)

> 'I've had it for quite a long time and you'd think by now I'd be able to keep it under control.... That's all they [health professionals] can do. As I say, they can only give me like medication, that's all they can do. They can't do nothing for it.' (White English man with long-term condition, 40-44 years)

However, there was also evidence that some individuals simply had a wider range of strategies for dealing with their health condition and greater 'mastery' (often deriving from experience) than others. Some respondents had become skilful at identifying their symptoms, monitoring their condition and knowing how to improve it. Individuals also talked about various practical strategies that they used to cope with their ill health and its associated complications such as having a fixed daily routine, writing things down to cope with memory loss, buying clothes that do not need to be ironed, cooking in large batches to reduce workload and so on.

> 'Stress brings it on and a lot of workload or if I'm picking up heavy things. And so what I do is, I sort of spread my work out now…. And if I can't do anything, I don't do it. I don't do it at all, I just leave it. If the house is a mess, it's a mess. If there's dishes to wash and they're left in the sink for two days, I don't do it.' (Pakistani woman with long-term condition, 45-49 years)

In addition to such problem-solving strategies, many respondents talked about needing to recognise when the situation cannot be within one's complete control. Here, mental strategies of coping and ways of relieving stress were felt to be most effective. A prominent theme was the importance of keeping busy and diverting the mind, as well as taking one day at a time.

Individuals who lacked such coping strategies tended to become totally consumed with the health condition, for instance spending extended periods of time worrying or at the other extreme being totally consumed by managing the condition and having no existence beyond it. As one White English woman, aged 54-59, put it, 'It sort of rules everything. It controls me'.

However, it was also evident that 'avoidance' strategies might have negative implications, reflecting a failure to adequately adjust to the implications of the health condition, as discussed above. Indeed, evidence of planning for the future was absent from most of our respondent stories, although this has been identified as an important dimension of resilience (Grant et al, 2007: forthcoming).

> 'I have not really thought what will happen in future…. I do not want to think about that…. Who knows what will happen! Maybe I go blind or just able to manage to walk about. Who knows?! Time will only tell. I feel scared when I think about it, so I do not want to think. I try living in the present and thank god for the day.' (Pakistani woman with long-term condition, 45-49 years)

A number of respondents found the unpredictability of their condition difficult to accept and felt constantly at risk and conscious of the possibility of death. Furthermore, an awareness of deterioration in their condition, and often the acquisition over time of multiple health complications, meant that a sense of control over the situation did not necessarily increase over time, as might be expected. As one Ghanaian female with a long-term condition, aged 50-54 years, put it: 'I'm really, really sick. I want to tell you that I think I'm dying…. Because I am in pain every time, I prefer to die with it, I don't want it anymore.'

Experiencing long delays in diagnosis and treatment appeared to undermine individuals' sense of control. Living with uncertainty was (or had been) extremely stressful for several respondents and had led them to 'put life on hold'. Moreover, the practical side of having to make multiple doctors visits often with no fixed pattern made it impossible for people to put in place daily routines and structures that could promote a feeling of control.

A further factor that was a characteristic of several respondents with high levels of emotional distress was a poor understanding of their condition and a feeling of powerlessness in relation to gaining information. Not surprisingly, this situation was more common for individuals with lower education and poor English language skills who were less able to access information effectively via health consultations, or independently via written materials, the internet and telephone helplines, sources mentioned by several other respondents.

> [Recounting a story of a failed attempt to understand his wife's condition and the treatment that she had received] 'You don't get a long time to discuss with your doctor. You have about 15-20 minutes to discuss and within those 15-20 minutes you have to discuss all that you want with them … I kept saying that I could not understand what was going on, and then my time with the doctor came to an end and I could not do anything and the interpreter who was there said that the doctor could not give me more time. And the doctor kept repeating that I was taking more time than allotted to me. So what could I do? I came back…. Now, who is going to find solutions to my problem?' (Bangladeshi man, family member, 40-44 years)

Holding understandings that linked ill health to externally located 'stresses' beyond one's control (such as difficult events in childhood or family disputes) also contributed to some individuals feeling lack of control over their condition. Although evident across all four communities, such explanations seemed particularly common among Bangladeshi and Pakistani women.

These findings are consistent with Charmaz's (2000) assertion that people need to learn what a health condition means in order to adapt to it. However, while Charmaz suggests that shared knowledge among patients can be a very valuable part of this, concerns about revealing their condition made many of our respondents ambivalent about talking openly with other individuals (a theme that is taken up in Chapter 6).

More generally, the close relationship with health services that many of our respondents had, implied a dependence upon others and a consequent risk of losing control. Furthermore, there was little evidence of individuals being offered strategies (whether practical or mental) to cope with their long-term condition. This in part reflects the low levels of involvement in ill-health-specific support groups, as we discuss in Chapter 6.

Support from other family members could help develop an individual's sense of control. However, consistency between family members' and the individual's own perceptions of the situation and appropriate action was again relevant here.

> 'There are many factors, but one has to cope. Secondly I have my family and my children with me, my, I mean, my Mrs. They also cope with me, when I am seriously sick they [unclear]. My younger daughter, you know, she looks after me. Sometimes it happens like this, because of sugar, my feet become very painful, the poor thing gives me massage. My wife becomes very worried, I think at least there is someone who worries for me, I am not alone, I am not alone. If something happens, someone will look after me.' (Pakistani man, family member with own long-term condition, 55-59 years)

Conclusions

Positively adapting to long-term ill health is an ongoing challenge for most individuals. While some of our respondents displayed resilience, many more appeared to be struggling to come to terms with their condition and had failed to reconcile ill health with a fulfilling life and a valued sense of self.

An emphasis on being 'normal' was prominent. Although striving to retain one's prior identity, roles and activities could be seen in some cases as positive, in other cases these actions led to unhappiness and clearly illustrated a failure to adjust mentally to having a long-term health condition. Furthermore, the strong pressure to hide ill health could mean that certain types of support were less forthcoming (either because the individual themselves or the potential providers of that support do not acknowledge a need).

It would seem then that all three dimensions (mental adjustment, self-worth and control) are important for resilience over the long term (although they do clearly interrelate quite closely). For instance, individuals who take their health condition on board without major disruption to their sense of self seem unlikely to retain 'buoyancy' and emotional well-being if they lack practical strategies for coping with their health condition on a day-to-day basis. On the other hand, those who are creative in their strategising, but lack the necessary inputs to achieve feelings of self-worth (for instance from family, friends or religious faith), may founder and lose the will to manage their condition, despite skills and experience.

Ethnicity was of relevance to the ways in which individuals experienced ill health, both because of expected behaviours and because of inclusion within ethnic social networks. However, we could not conclude from our data that any particular ethnic identity implied higher or lower chances of 'resilience' in the face of ill health. Nevertheless, there were some indications of the types of support that might be most needed and effective. For instance, Bangladeshi and Pakistani women appeared to be most likely to need support in developing feelings of self-worth, and religious faith may be an appropriate avenue through which to strengthen this dimension for many. Ghanaian women who were living alone often lacked family members who could provide practical support (see Chapter 6) and might therefore need help in developing creative strategies for dealing with the limitations brought on by ill health. In relation to gender, there was evidence to suggest that men found it more difficult than women to adjust to new, non-working roles, and therefore to find meaning in life where ill health brings incapacity (although here the older Pakistani and Bangladeshi men did appear to have an advantage over the White English and Ghanaians). Gaining a sense of control seemed particularly difficult for many of our respondents, and may be an area where individuals with ongoing, unpredictable and often deteriorating health conditions need particular support. Forward planning, in particular, seemed lacking in many of our respondents, but is something that could be relatively easily supported by service interventions.

A further point that needs emphasising is the diversity of 'outcomes' that may constitute 'resilience' (or positive adaptation). For some, giving up certain roles and activities, including paid employment, or becoming used to new roles, was appropriate. The following chapters explore in more detail how these diverse responses to long-term ill health influenced attitudes towards and access to employment (Chapter 4), receipt of benefits (Chapter 5) and social participation and the support that it provided (Chapter 6).

Long-term health conditions and employment

SUMMARY POINTS

- Both minority ethnicity and long-term ill health are associated with greatly reduced chances of employment for both men and women.
- Respondents with long-term ill health expressed a commitment to paid work and recognition of its benefits, over and above income. However, there was variation in the extent to which paid work was seen as a possibility or priority.
- While there were differences in the ways in which relationships between paid work and ill health were discussed between the ethnic groups, quantitative analysis showed no ethnic differences in the effect of ill health on employment.
- Ethnic penalties in employment were, however, substantial and resulted in much lower rates of employment for those from the three minority groups, than among otherwise comparable White British men and women.
- Risks of unemployment were also significantly higher for Pakistani and Black African women compared with their White British counterparts.
- Respondents identified diverse barriers to employment: their inability following ill health to return to former types of employment (particularly that which was physically demanding); the demands of hospital appointments and the experience of chronic pain; employers' inflexibility; and, particularly for those with mental health conditions, stigma and discrimination.
- Pay was also affected both by having an activity-limiting health condition and by ethnicity. Pay deficits were particularly large for working Bangladeshi men. Both Bangladeshi men and White British men (and, to a lesser extent, White British women) experienced lower pay if they had a long-term health condition.
- Ethnic pay penalties were found for men and for Pakistani women regardless of health status, and Bangladeshi and Black African women without a long-term health condition were also penalised. However, the highly selected group of Bangladeshi and Black African working women with an activity-limiting condition were not disadvantaged in pay compared with White British women.

Introduction

We know a lot about ethnic differences in employment rates, and labour market disadvantage and its association with ethnicity. For example, work by Blackaby et al (1999, 2002, 2005) has continued to reveal the existence of an ethnic penalty in employment in relation to both pay and employment rates (see also Heath and Cheung, 2006). There is also an extensive literature concerning employment disadvantage, ill health and disability (for instance, Bartley and Lewis, 2002). For example, Burchardt (2000a) described the 'economic exclusion' of disabled people, and Berthoud (2006) reported employment rates of under 30% (compared with an overall rate of 76%).[11] Smith and Twomey (2002) identified four reasons why labour market disadvantage might arise for those with a disability: severity of the disability (which we have shown in Chapter 3 to have a large subjective element); workplace access; discrimination; and relative returns from employment and from benefit. To these it is important to add household factors: demands of caring and juggling care.

Nevertheless, the ways in which ethnicity and long-term health conditions operate together in producing employment disadvantage has been less fully explored. A few studies have examined the effects of ethnicity and health using the LFS (Berthoud, 2003), the General Household Survey (Berthoud and Blekesaune, 2006) and the Census (Clark and Drinkwater, 2005). But, while these studies indicate that there may well be no differences in the effects of ill health on labour market outcomes across ethnic groups, there remains scope for exploring this question in more detail.

In this chapter, using the LFS, we explore the question of the joint effects of health status and ethnic group on employment outcomes. We use a tailored measure of long-term health condition, created from consecutive waves of the survey (see 'Methods' in Chapter 1), and we look at differences in both employment and unemployment. We examine whether the effect of having a long-term health condition on chances of employment or unemployment varies according to the ethnic group of the person with the condition. Presenting descriptive analyses initially, we investigate this question controlling for a range of other 'risk' factors for labour market participation, such as lower educational qualifications. Furthermore, we integrate this analysis with our qualitative data to shed light on the links between long-term health conditions and the labour market and to consider whether these are experienced differently across the ethnic groups.

Illness trajectories and attitudes to employment

Our life-history-taking approach to the in-depth interviews allowed us to explore in some detail the ways in which health conditions and employment were related across time for each individual. There were varied patterns, but commonly onset of the health condition was not experienced as a sudden event, but as gradual and intermittent. Many respondents had experienced multiple health conditions over many years and had experienced periods of employment and unemployment as well as periods of sickness-related leave/benefit receipt. Thus, consistent with other research (Burchardt, 2000b; Jenkins and Rigg, 2004) the health conditions were not usually fixed states, the impact on employment could precede clear recognition of incapacity, and changes in both health and employment status could track each other, and be reversed.

Some of our respondents who were not in employment had reached a point at which the labour market felt distant to them, and certainly respondents' narratives accorded with analyses that suggest the longer a person is out of the labour market, the less likely it is that they will re-enter it. While for some this related to a downwards spiralling in mood and motivation (Chapter 3), for others this withdrawal from the labour market could be seen as a pragmatic response to worsening health, and in some cases was accompanied by taking on other fulfilling roles (such as voluntary work or being an active grandparent).

Notwithstanding these patterns, in common with earlier work (Alcock et al, 2003; Easterlow and Smith, 2003), many of our respondents, whether working or not, expressed positive

---

[11] This differs somewhat from the rate identified by Smith and Twomey (2002) of 48% (compared with an overall rate of 81%) but the sources and, more importantly, the definitions of disability varied fundamentally between the two. See the discussion of this point in Chapter 1.

attitudes to work. Work was seen to offer a variety of benefits over and above providing an income including: giving the individual a purpose and meaning in life; providing a daily routine; distracting the mind from illness symptoms; creating an opportunity for friendships and socialising; and providing independence and control over the individual's life. Non-employment was often regarded as a serious source of frustration. As a Ghanaian woman with a long-term condition, aged 50-55 years, explained: 'Because it's boring staying home on your own.... If you go back to work it puts you back into society'.

Respondents often displayed great determination and creativity in managing their health condition alongside their working lives, reflecting the importance given to the working role by many.

'I remember I used to work – do some selling in the market – I had to use hot water bottle beside me all the time, otherwise when you get cold – by the time you get home you're sick already.' (Ghanaian woman with long-term condition, 45-49 years)

However, across all four groups, further discussion often highlighted a range of 'qualifiers' to this general positive orientation. Work was not always regarded as good for health and well-being: stress and the physical nature of jobs were highlighted in this regard. Several respondents also mentioned that they had in practice gained little job satisfaction in the past. Conflicts between work and other roles and activities, particularly caring roles, were also regularly highlighted. Our qualitative work also suggested some important variations by ethnicity, age/life cycle and gender in the extent to which paid employment was felt to be a central component of self-identity (see the section on barriers to employment and Chapter 5).

We turn now to consider in more detail the patterns of employment and economic activity and their associations with long-term health conditions and ethnicity.

Ill health, economic activity and employment

Labour market analyses often focus on those actually in paid employment and contrast this status to the combined group of those who are unemployed (actively seeking paid work) and those who are economically inactive (not employed and not seeking work). For some analysts, differences in such employment rates illustrate employment disadvantage across differing characteristics (Clark and Drinkwater, 2005; Berthoud and Blekesaune, 2006). However, others focus on the specific disadvantage associated with *unemployment* (Blackaby et al, 1997), drawing a distinction between economic inactivity, which may constitute a preference and unemployment, which is clearly undesired. We consider all three possible states: employment, unemployment and economic inactivity, in order to understand the complexity of the relationship between labour market outcomes, ethnicity and ill health.

Figure 3 summarises rates of employment, unemployment and economic inactivity by ethnic group and health status for men, while Figure 4 covers women. Employment was lower among those reporting a long-term health condition and yet lower again among those with an activity-limiting health condition for all groups and across the sexes. However, there were clear differences by ethnic group within each health status.

White British men had the highest employment rates and the lowest unemployment rates across all health statuses. While high proportions of minority ethnic men with long-term health conditions reported economic inactivity, nevertheless substantial proportions were also unemployed. Even among those with an activity-limiting condition the rates of

Figure 3: Employment, unemployment and economic inactivity by ethnic group and health status: men

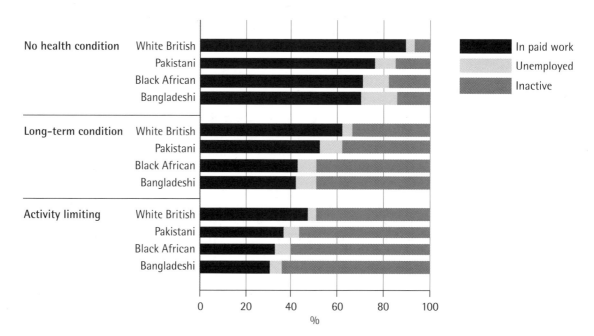

Notes: Proportions are adjusted by person weights.
Source: LFS, pooled quarters, 2002-05

Figure 4: Employment, unemployment and economic inactivity by ethnic group and health status: women

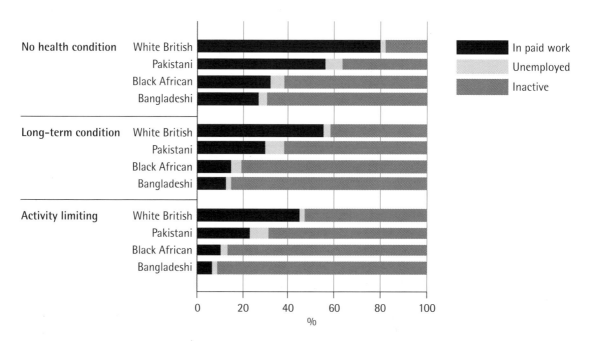

Notes: Proportions are adjusted by person weights.
Source: LFS, pooled quarters, 2002-05

unemployment for minority ethnic men were substantially higher than those for White British men. For these unemployed men, long-term ill health had not been translated into economic inactivity; they were still actively looking for work. These patterns accord with the qualitative finding that work formed a central component of male self-identity for the majority across all four ethnic groups.

Turning to the women, the two aspects of Figure 4 that stand out are the much higher employment rates of White British women at all three health statuses and the high unemployment rates of Black African women, again at all three health statuses. The former indicates that while ill health does reduce labour market participation for White British women, a substantial proportion are nevertheless able to remain in paid work. The latter suggests a clear work orientation regardless of health (and despite the relatively low achieved employment rates) that was clearly evident among the Ghanaian women in our qualitative work. Among Pakistani and Bangladeshi women, having an activity-limiting health condition corresponded to inactivity for the vast majority. This is likely to represent a combination of constraints and preferences, which converge to make paid employment at best an unattractive option and commonly something that has not been considered at all, particularly post-marriage. Nevertheless, we did come across some Bangladeshi and Pakistani women being creative and resourceful in taking opportunities for paid work. We also found variation at the individual level as to whether ill health and employment were perceived as compatible or not (see Chapter 3), with one Bangladeshi woman managing to maintain her job in the face of ill health by going home at lunchtimes to lie down.

Overall then, we can see that having a long-term health condition and an activity-limiting condition in particular corresponds to a systematic decrease in employment across ethnic groups, with a corresponding increase in economic inactivity. Differences in levels of ill health did not appear to account for ethnic differences in employment. Instead, at each health status, White British men and women were more likely to be employed than those from the other groups. For men, unemployment rates decreased among those with a long-term or activity-limiting health condition, suggesting that some who would have been unemployed if not experiencing a long-term health condition became economically inactive if they did. However, substantial proportions remain unemployed, implying continued labour market engagement despite the obstacles of ill health. Rates of unemployment were higher for minority ethnic groups at all three health statuses. Thus, the combination of ill health and ethnic employment disadvantage does not necessarily translate into disengagement from the labour market through economic inactivity. Among women, unemployment rates were constant across the three health statuses for all groups. This means that Black African women, whether with a long-term health condition or not, faced particularly high unemployment risks.

In the next section, we examine in more depth the relative contribution of ill health, ethnicity and other factors (such as qualifications and local labour market) to the patterns of employment, unemployment and economic inactivity described here.

Ill health, ethnicity or other factors?

We now turn to multivariate analysis to evaluate the particular contribution of ill health (considered in terms of whether the person had a long-term health condition, whether it was activity limiting, and number of conditions) to chances of employment, unemployment and economic inactivity, holding constant characteristics that are relevant to employment status.[12] Here we summarise the main results for men and women and illustrate them with predicted probabilities for particular sets of characteristics.[13]

---

[12] Variables included were age and age squared to capture possibly non-linear effects of age, educational qualifications, unemployment rate for each region at each time point, housing tenure, length of time spent in the UK (if not born in the UK) and whether married/partnered, with a child under five and region.

[13] We used multinomial logistic regression models to estimate the effects on the three outcomes of employment, unemployment and economic activity relative to each other. Full tables for these and the other models referred to in this chapter are available from the authors on request.

For men, activity-limiting illness had a fairly strong negative effect on employment probabilities. The number of conditions also decreased the probability of employment. Being Pakistani, Bangladeshi or Black African also had a negative impact on employment probabilities over and above health status (and the other control variables). That is, the clear ethnic differences observed in Figure 3 were not explained by differences in age, local unemployment rates, educational qualifications and so on. We summarised these ethnic group and ill health effects using simulations. We compared the predicted employment rates for individuals with activity-limiting illness from each of the minority ethnic groups with the predicted employment rates that they would have if they were White British and did not have a long-term health condition (but all other characteristics remained the same). This allows us to see (in a way that regression coefficients cannot show us) the large employment disadvantage resulting from minority ethnicity and health status jointly.

Figure 5 shows these predicted rates for Pakistani men. In the left half of the figure, the employment probabilities for those with an activity-limiting health condition follow a curve with age, but are mainly low across the whole age range. This contrasts dramatically with the right-hand side of the figure, which removes the disadvantage associated both with 'being Pakistani' and with having an activity-limiting health condition, but *leaves all other characteristics* (such as educational qualifications) as they occur among Pakistani men. We see now that the majority have employment probabilities of between 70% and 100%, especially those aged up to their mid-forties.

The patterns for Bangladeshi and Black African men with activity-limiting ill health were similar to those for Pakistani men. That is, their employment chances would jump from

Figure 5: Predicted probabilities of employment for Pakistani men with an activity-limiting long-term health condition, and for the same men 'as if' White British and without a long-term health condition

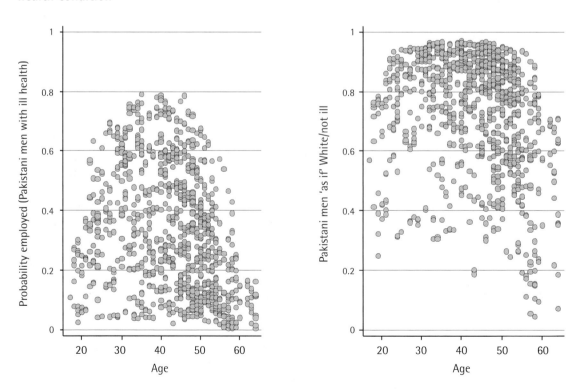

Notes: Predicted probabilities based on multinomial logistic regression, with person weights. 'Ill' is shorthand for long-term health condition.
Source: LFS, pooled quarters, 2002-05

being predominantly under 50% to being predominantly over 50% – and over 90% at prime ages, if they were White British and had no ill health (but all other characteristics remained the same). This shows us, importantly, that tackling the employment disadvantage associated with ethnicity and that associated with long-term ill health would massively improve the employment chances of minority ethnic men, regardless of interventions related to skills or local labour markets.

For women, results were broadly comparable with those for men: the effects of ill health and of ethnic group showed similar direction, size and significance of effects. That is, activity-limiting ill health and number of health conditions were associated with reduced chances of employment and increased probabilities of unemployment and economic inactivity, holding other relevant characteristics constant. Being of Pakistani, Bangladeshi and Black African ethnicity significantly reduced chances of being in employment, relative to White British women, increased risks of economic inactivity, and, for Pakistani and Black African women, increased risks of unemployment.

Thus, we see that health status has a marked impact on employment status for all women. Interestingly, the impact of ill health was as strong for men as it was for women. Our qualitative data suggested that non-participation in employment could present a more acceptable option for women than for men, given the availability of alternative roles within the household. However, on the other hand, part-time, flexible, often service-sector or childcare-related jobs that are more compatible with the obstacles posed by chronic ill health (particularly pain, fatigue and needing time off) were perceived to be more accessible to women. As the quantitative models illustrate, such 'gendered' processes did not translate into significantly different effects of ill health on employment between the sexes.

But women from the minority ethnic groups faced additional employment disadvantage that cannot be explained by having less 'employable' characteristics. The higher risks of unemployment for Black African and Pakistani women, relative to White British women, are also worthy of note. These women were actively seeking work, and had not translated the obstacles they faced to paid employment into an acceptance of economic inactivity.

Barriers to employment

Clearly, across all four ethnic groups and across both men and women, having a long-term health condition has a large and significant impact on the chances of being employed, particularly if the condition is one that limits daily activities. We turn now to consider what light our qualitative data can throw on the processes contributing to this disadvantage.

Virtually across the board, respondents who had spent some time out of work found it difficult to re-enter employment. Respondents' stories often revealed multiple short periods of work interspersed with periods of inactivity or job seeking, reflecting the intermittent and unpredictable nature of many of the health conditions and the difficulty many people faced in sustaining employment over a long period of time. Furthermore, in general, the health condition was just one factor among multiple issues that made re-entry into work difficult.

Many respondents who were out of work identified their physical limitations and impairments as direct obstacles to employment and often expressed sentiments such as 'I wouldn't employ me', suggesting that they acknowledged their lower productivity and liability for employers. That said, few respondents expressed the feeling that they were incapable of performing any kind of work at all because of their illness (consistent with earlier work, for example Beatty and Fothergill, 2002). More commonly, people talked about being unable to perform 'heavy work' (such as work that involved lifting, factory-based work or work that involved standing up for long periods of time) or identified particular types of activity that would be difficult for them. However, limited education, skills and experience and intermittent work histories meant that 'light' jobs (often perceived to be office-based jobs where much of the work could be performed sitting down) were often inaccessible. Furthermore, many respondents identified pain, fatigue and the unpredictability of symptoms as factors that seriously compromised their ability to perform many types of job. A further important factor was the burden of medical appointments, for some respondents several per month, requiring an unacceptably high level of absenteeism.

> 'If I get a job I can't work because I have got too many appointment at the hospital – too many appointment. You can't get a job like that. Nobody give you job like that. Five, six different departments I have to visit.' (Bangladeshi man with long-term condition, 30-34 years)

> 'There was a shop-fitting job. I do three or four days maybe, shop-fitting job lasted a week and a bit and then I just [pause]. I was swallowing painkillers like nobody's business and I did about a month's worth of painkillers in a week and a half. My doctor went mad at me! And then I said 'no'. I just couldn't do it.' (White English man with long-term condition, 40-44 years)

A further factor that seemed to contribute to the probability of remaining out of work was the tendency for some respondents to consider only a very narrow range of options, often focusing on the jobs that they had performed in the past, and relying on word of mouth for information about job opportunities. While evident among a number of respondents in the White English, Bangladeshi and Pakistani groups, our Ghanaian respondents seemed more open to a wider range of possibilities and to face fewer proscriptions against particular types of work, and a greater willingness to retrain, perhaps reflecting their more diverse socioeconomic profile.

Respondents' stories across all the groups also suggested heavy reliance on informal routes to finding employment and negative perceptions of Job Centre Plus and related employment agencies.

> [Talking about a failed attempt to gain work though a specialised Job Centre scheme] 'They've stopped that scheme, but as I say it was so incompetently handled it wasn't any good. Every so often they have disability advisers in but you never see the same person twice…. At the same time, they then … they put you on this scheme for long-term unemployed run by Reed employment agencies. They then kicked me off that for not being fit enough to work.' (White English man with long-term condition, 40-44 years)

> [Talking about her attempts to set up her own business] 'You end up losing. But then they always say 'Oh going back to work, we will help you'. As soon as you start they cut off everything, you know, and they leave you just like that…. It's unfair.' (Ghanaian woman with long-term condition, 45-49 years)

The attitudes and practices of employers and managers also had a significant effect on the ability to remain in, or re-enter, employment, for some. Having a supportive work environment had been very important in helping some respondents remain in work despite long-term ill health, and even taking extended periods of sick leave. However, work scenarios were very variable, and in a number of cases the same individual had experienced very different treatment at different times during their history of ill health. Not surprisingly, better-qualified individuals in more secure jobs appeared to receive greater support and were able to be more flexible in the ways in which they combined work with their ill-health-related related needs (such as taking time off for appointments, working from home or having a gradual return to work).

'When I came at first [to the UK] and I was well [I worked] but not now. I can't do it because I am ill all the time. And with this kind of [cleaning] work nobody will hold it for you because of your pressure [that is, illness].' (Ghanaian woman with long-term condition, 50-54 years)

'I didn't go back to work full time straightaway. I went back on a part-time basis ... and gradually building up the hours.... And I've got to tell you that before I went back to work the director of the branch where I was actually sent round a note to everybody ... and he said something like 'C is returning to work on such-and-such a day [with impairment] while she waits for the operation, um, it is important', and he stressed the important, 'that you do not make her feel alienated in any way or form'. Which I thought was really good.' (White English woman with long-term condition, 40-44 years)

In a number of cases, working respondents expressed the feeling that employers did not trust their employees, were unsympathetic to those with ill health, and that sickness absence or low productivity would result in sacking. Such factors tended to encourage individuals to conceal their illness, to avoid taking time off sick wherever possible, and in at least one case, to stop working without any consultation with the employer regarding the ill health and related needs.

'Everything you do now, you have to care for in a year, I don't go more than 13 days sick. If I go more than 13 days sick then I get a big problem, then I go to the [employer's name] medical board [titters humourlessly]. They ask me the questions that why are you sick blah blah blah.... If you go again sick they sign down, because you are unfit to do the job, you know, and they give the sack.' (Pakistani man, family member with own health condition, 55-59 years)

A number of respondents had been forced to leave their jobs. For some this came as a relief, since they had been struggling to combine work with ill health for a long period of time, or they were unhappy in the job. Others, however, felt that their dismissal was unfair and discriminatory, reflecting the employer's unwillingness to make allowances for their health condition.

'So before when [the nurse] call me they say this is what they are proposing to you, they want to make you redundant. They would pay me because I couldn't use my arm properly now. I said well I just want to do three days a week, I didn't say I want to quit. I love working because if I go home and sit down what am I going to do ... I want to stay and do three days till I get better then I'll do full time.... I got in touch with ACAS. After the two weeks, I went back and said 'OK, if they want to make me redundant give me some money, why not?' Let me take it because I don't want to drag it. I'm not that strong to drag it and then going to court.' (Ghanaian woman with long-term condition, 50-54 years)

In terms of seeking new employment, some respondents across all the ethnic groups also identified discrimination by employers as a barrier.

Interviewer: 'What's your impression been of the employers?'

Respondent: 'Get out! [Laughs] Why would we want to give you a job?!' (White English man with long-term condition, 40-44 years)

As well as concerns about direct discrimination, many respondents expressed fears about revealing their health condition to potential employers and lacked confidence in being able to perform adequately. Again, the unpredictability of symptoms was a prominent concern for many. For some, prolonged periods of inactivity had clearly undermined their self-esteem and made work seem a remote possibility.

> 'I was down, that's what my doctor said, according to depression I was down. I don't eat, I can't sleep and I was thinking how can I get a job and what is hanging over my head because I can't go back to work and tell them I got cancer. That's why I lost my job. Who take you? No one will take you. I didn't try even. I know that … because I was in [depression] so how would I have confidence to [apply for work]?' (Ghanaian woman with long-term condition, 50-54 years)

Thus, despite the fact that many of our respondents' stories revealed the ways in which wider society, and particularly employers, placed obstacles in the way of their securing work, few individuals challenged such rejection or sought to actively claim their right to employment. Very few of our respondents showed any understanding of their rights under disability discrimination legislation. In this way it can be seen that the so-called 'social model of disability' did not resonate strongly with many of our respondents. Instead, most individuals talked of guilt and worry, and saw their health condition, rather than society, as the source of their difficulty in finding employment.

Several respondents had engaged in voluntary work as a way of gaining experience, keeping skills up to date, or making a slower transition back into the world of work. In some cases, this seemed to be an effective strategy, especially where the individual had prior work experience. However, it is important to note that for many individuals voluntary work did not lead to paid employment, often, they felt, because voluntary work is not considered by employers to be 'proper' work experience.

Decisions about whether to remain in the labour force or not were also importantly affected by family/household context. While several female respondents had chosen to combine income-earning, household maintenance and childrearing roles while fully fit, the onset of ill health had forced them to reconsider their priorities. Fatigue was a significant factor for many of our respondents and one that reduced the number of hours in the day for active work. A number of women with long-term conditions had switched from full-time to part-time work or stopped work altogether because they felt working was compromising the quality of care they could give to their children. Importantly, this was a concern for those with older children as well as those with younger ones, with mothers stressing the importance of having time to talk to their children and help with homework. Such concerns were heightened for single parents.

> 'I decided no, this work is too stressful for me, and I didn't have time for the children. By the time I come back I'll see I'm really tired, I can't even help them with their homework.' (Ghanaian woman with long-term condition, 45-49 years)

Some individuals felt able to stop work because there were other sources of income to the household, and in some cases because they viewed their income as additional, rather than primary. Among White English families, since it was common for both men and women to be working, some respondents were able to 'fall back' on their spouse's earnings. In contrast, many Ghanaian respondents seemed particularly vulnerable in this respect since marital breakdown was common and families were often split between Ghana, the UK and other countries. As discussed above, it was relatively uncommon for Bangladeshi and Pakistani women to have work experience so that the withdrawal from employment of a husband due to long-term ill health could not easily be substituted for (see Chapter 2).

Exploring the possibility of differential effects of ill health

The discussion of the qualitative data above, as well as the presentation of quantitative and qualitative data in the previous chapters, has pointed towards some differences between the ethnic groups that may mean that when ill health arises, the ability and motivation to stay in work, or to (re)gain it, may differ. In particular, there was evidence for differences in attitudes towards employment, particularly among women and at older ages, concentration within different sectors of work and heavy reliance on intra-ethnic information networks, as well as some differences in patterns of caring and home responsibilities across groups. However, many commonalities across the groups were also highlighted, as well complexities, so that these differences between the groups did not necessarily all act in the same direction. Thus, although the qualitative data suggest the relevance of ethnicity for the ways in which individual ill health is experienced, it is less clear what ethnic group differences, if any, may exist in terms of how of ill health impacts on employment prospects.

In addition, we found some evidence that the impact of ill health on employment prospects among our, relatively disadvantaged, sample related to the more limited options presented by particular sets of skills, experience and qualifications. Managing to remain in work seemed to be more possible in non-manual forms of work, both because of the nature of the work and, possibly, the extent of flexibility and support. Moreover, the financial returns to such work made it more possible to avoid the benefits trap in such jobs.[14] Indeed, some respondents explicitly discussed this issue: 'I mean it was such a poorly paid job what I was doing in the warehouse job ... I mean I don't think it works out. It didn't work out an awful lot more than what I'm getting now' (White English man with long-term condition, 40-44 years). Such considerations related not just to whether respondents calculated that they would be better off in work, but also to their fear of the transitionary period and to a lack of trust in the benefits system. They described past experiences of having to battle for what they have got and not wanting to risk losing it, especially if paying off debts. On the other hand, for other respondents, financial constraints meant that not working was not regarded as an option.

Clearly, there is the potential for the impact of ill health on employment to vary between population subgroups, and it is of particular interest to explore whether ill health enhanced the employment disadvantage we already observed for minority ethnic groups – or indeed, whether ill health was less significant in its effects given existing penalties and employment disadvantage. We therefore explored these potential differences in the impact of ill health according to ethnicity and educational qualifications using the quantitative data.[15]

Our investigations clearly indicated that there were no differences in the effects of ill health across the different ethnic groups. This was the case for both men and women. Thus, the impact of ill health, discussed under 'Ill health, economic activity and employment' above, was neither greater nor smaller for any particular group. This is an important finding since it suggests that addressing employment disadvantage associated with long-term ill health will affect all groups equally and substantially improve employment chances across the

---

[14] The ways that tax credits intersect with Housing Benefit mean that the benefits trap is most likely to be an issue for those in rented accommodation – either council or privately rented. And, clearly, the size of rents tends to be a particular issue in London compared with the rest of the country.

[15] We tested for these effects in a number of ways, investigating simply the probability of employment rather than multiple outcomes for this analysis. We inspected the coefficients for interaction effects in linear probability models; explored the estimates and confidence intervals for predicted probabilities from logistic regression models at different points on the distribution of employment probabilities; and ran separate models by ethnic group, testing for the equality of the coefficients for the illness variables across the models. We also ran linear probability models for the groups separately and tested the interaction between illness and education across these.

board. Conversely, addressing employment disadvantage associated with long-term ill health will not mitigate the employment disadvantage associated with minority ethnicity.

However, when we looked at whether the effects of ill health varied by the level of educational qualifications, as speculated, we did observe an effect. Thus, those with a long-term health condition but high qualifications were less disadvantaged relative to those without a long-term health condition but similarly qualified. Those with low qualifications and a long-term health condition were more disadvantaged relative to those without a long-term health condition but a similar lack of qualifications. Thus, addressing levels of qualifications among those with long-term health conditions may reduce the big impact of ill health on employment chances. However, we have to be cautious in making such an assumption since it may still be hard for those with a long-term health condition to re-enter employment: those with higher levels of qualifications may find it easier to remain in their existing job – or move sideways. Once they have left the labour market their qualifications may not count for so much. In addition, such a conclusion does not allow for the fact that the condition may have been produced or exacerbated by the particular job. Nevertheless, the role of skills and qualifications clearly has an important bearing on the relationship between health condition and employment.

These differences in the impact of long-term ill health according to educational qualifications were consistent across all the minority ethnic groups except for Black African men and Pakistani women. For these latter two groups it appeared that the effects of ill health were consistent across levels of qualifications.[16]

However, the extent to which qualification levels affected the impact of ill health was relatively minor. Overall then, while increasing skills levels has an important role to play in improving employment chances, the particular advantage it will have for those with a long-term health condition is small compared with the impact of ill health itself.

The financial rewards of work

It has been frequently argued that ethnic penalties in pay are less significant than ethnic penalties in employment (for example, Clark and Drinkwater, 2005). However, the raw differences in rates of pay remain stark (Platt, 2006). Figures 6 and 7 show average earnings by health status for men and women from the different groups. While the figure for men shows lower wages for those with a long-term or activity-limiting condition, the differences were not as substantial as the ethnic group variations; and there seemed to be little variation for women. Ethnic penalties in pay were found even for the highly selected group who were both long-term ill and in employment. (Figures 3 and 4 showed the low rates of employment among those of minority ethnicity with a long-term health condition.)

However, these averages include both full-time and part-time earnings and part-time earnings are substantially lower than full-time earnings (Olsen and Walby, 2004; Manning and Petrongolo, 2005; Platt, 2006). These averages are therefore potentially misleading if there are large differences in patterns of part-time earning by health status as well as ethnic group and sex. On the other hand, the inclusion of part-time work may be appropriate if ill health means that part-time work becomes a more feasible option than full-time work. In fact, excluding part-time workers[17] made little difference to the overall pattern between groups and across health status. Figure 6 shows a particularly strong impact of long-term ill

---

[16] This will be related to the fact that there was a preponderance of higher qualifications among Black African men and of lower (or no) qualifications among Pakistani women.

[17] Figures are available from the authors on request.

Figure 6: Average hourly pay by ethnic group and health status: men

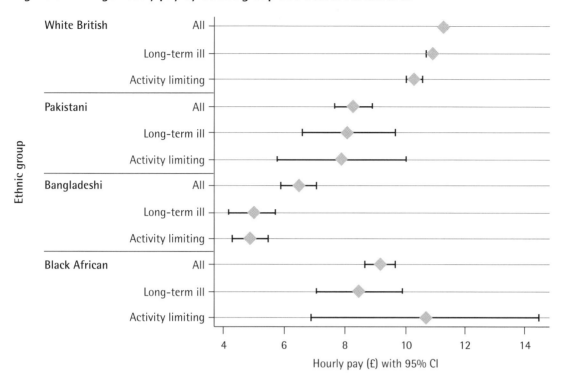

Notes: Person income weights used. Hourly wages have been adjusted by the consumer price index and set at 2005 prices. 'Ill' is shorthand for having a long-term health condition. 95% confidence intervals (CIs) shown.
Source: LFS, wave 1, pooled quarters, 2001-05

Figure 7: Average hourly pay by ethnic group and health status: women

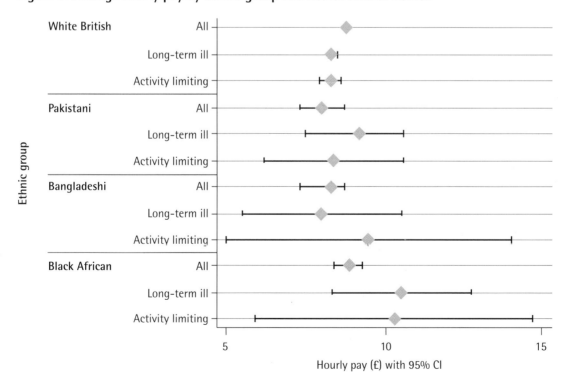

Notes: Person income weights used. Hourly wages have been adjusted by the consumer price index and set at 2005 prices. 'Ill' is shorthand for having a long-term health condition. 95% confidence intervals (CIs) shown.
Source: LFS, wave 1, pooled quarters, 2001-05

health on the pay of Bangladeshi men, and there was also a clear effect for White British men and a smaller one for White British women (Figure 7). There did not appear to be a clear relationship between long-term ill health and pay for the other groups of men and women.

How do we understand these patterns of pay? Are the differences between ethnic groups significant? And can they be attributed to characteristics or contexts that tend to command lower wages? Is there a significant impact of health condition on pay? Turning again to multivariate analysis to investigate these questions, we investigated the effect of ethnic group on pay for men and women, controlling for relevant characteristics.[18] We found that, among men, there was a large negative effect on pay of being of Bangladeshi, Pakistani or Black African ethnicity, controlling for the various other factors including health status. Having an activity-limiting health condition and the number of health conditions also had a negative and significant effect on pay – but the size of the effect was much smaller. Thus, ethnic group is much more important to the amount of pay you command than your health status *for those in employment*. For those who were both of a minority ethnicity and had an activity-limiting health condition, their financial rewards from work were low.

Among women, pay of Bangladeshi, Pakistani and Black African women is lower than that of White British women holding other characteristics constant, although the size of the difference was not as great as for men. Having an activity-limiting health condition and the number of conditions also reduced pay, although, as for men, the size of the impact was relatively small compared with other factors, including ethnicity.

We also investigated whether the reduction in pay associated with having an activity-limiting health condition varied by ethnic group. For men there appeared to be no difference. For women, the association between ill health and pay did vary by ethnic group for certain groups. All minority ethnic women without a long-term health condition were disadvantaged relative to their White British counterparts. However, Black African and Bangladeshi women with an activity-limiting illness were not disadvantaged in pay relative to comparable White British women. Such women are a very select group, having overcome the joint barriers of ethnic disadvantage and ill health to enter employment in the first place. Once employed, they appeared to command pay on a par with their White British counterparts. It is interesting, however, that this was not the case for the Pakistani women.

As a general point, where there is considerable variation in the proportions who are in the labour market across the sexes or between the groups, it is reasonable to suppose that those who are in paid employment are going to be particularly well equipped to succeed in the labour market, relative to those who choose or are constrained to be unemployed or inactive. This means that the pay rates that we observe do not represent the potential reward to work for all those currently out of work. Instead, potential pay from employment for those currently not in work is likely to be somewhat lower.[19]

---

[18] We used OLS and took the log of hourly earnings as our dependent variable and controlled for similar variables as in our earlier models of economic activity, adding some aspects of the workplace context itself (the industry of the job, whether the job is permanent or in some way impermanent, whether it is in the public sector or the private sector). Regression tables are available from the authors on request.

[19] We undertook some preliminary investigation of such 'selection effects' using appropriate statistical approaches, but the results were inconclusive. That is, it was not clear that those out of the labour market would receive substantially lower wages if they were in work than those already in work. However, these findings merit further investigation.

Conclusions

This chapter addressed the joint effects of ethnic group and health status on the employment situation of men and women. It found that the effects were indeed joint: both minority ethnicity and having a long-term health condition decreased the chances of employment and increased the chances of unemployment and economic inactivity. Similar effects were also observed in relation to pay for those in employment, although the impact of ill health on pay was much smaller. The analysis did not reveal variation in the effects of ill health across the ethnic groups. Thus, the impact of ill health on employment was constant regardless of ethnicity. This contrasts with the differences across groups in the ways that people spoke about employment and ill health in our qualitative work. However, substantial ethnic penalties in employment, for those both with and without long-term health conditions, shape the context from which our respondents assess their ill health and its relation to the labour market. Our findings indicate that interventions to address both health-related employment penalties and ethnic employment penalties are necessary if those suffering the greatest levels of employment disadvantage are to benefit. They will not be reached by focusing on one approach alone.

Moreover, the poor rewards in work for certain groups, particularly Bangladeshi men, need to be considered when the benefits of employment are being promoted. Such low levels of financial rewards for those who do manage to gain and retain paid work, despite ill health, raises questions about the ability of paid work to raise people out of poverty. The additional benefits of work, besides the economic ones, are stressed in policy and were recognised by our respondents. However, they also indicated how paid work can bring stresses and complications, and can impact negatively as well as positively on health status. Supporting people with a long-term health condition to move into employment requires, then, adequate consideration of both the type of job they can secure and its levels of pay. In addition, adequate support is needed for those for whom work is not the optimum solution. There is clearly a role of the skills agenda in improving both chances of work and pay across ethnic groups, especially for those with a long-term health condition. However, again, this needs to be addressed alongside the issues of long-term ill health and ethnic employment disadvantage. On its own, improving skills and qualifications will not tackle the employment penalties of the most disadvantaged.

5

Long-term health conditions and welfare benefits

SUMMARY POINTS

- Given low levels of employment among individuals with long-term ill health, income replacement benefits, and benefits aimed at offsetting additional expenditure, may play a crucial role in reducing economic hardship.
- Current policy directives and public opinion would suggest that both deciding to claim and the award of such benefits is straightforward.
- However, evidence shows that receipt of such benefits is often well below maximum and that minority ethnic individuals may face particular obstacles, although detailed investigation of people's experiences of claiming is lacking.
- For many of our respondents the decision to claim 'sickness' benefits was not taken lightly, and the claiming process was stressful and time-consuming.
- Just 19% of those with an activity-limiting long-term condition received Disability Living Allowance. Pakistani, Bangladeshi and Black African individuals had much lower receipt than comparable White British individuals.
- Our quantitative analyses also suggested striking differences in receipt of Incapacity Benefit by ethnicity, with White British men having the highest proportions in receipt (55%) and Bangladeshi men the lowest (just 27%).
- Respondents across all four ethnic groups held concerns about the undesirability of claiming ill-health-related benefits that were related to the perceived negative implications of assuming the identity of 'unfit for work' or 'disabled'. Such concerns were particularly strong among the Ghanaians.
- However, limited access to information and specialist support appeared to be much more significant obstacles, and ones that were heightened for many of the minority ethnic individuals. Ethnically dominated social networks resulted in differential access to information and 'know-how'.
- Receiving Incapacity Benefit/Income Support does not, in and of itself, appear to exclude people from the labour market. However, some recipients felt outside 'mainstream' society and expressed strong preferences for (re)-entering the world of work.
- Nevertheless, some Incapacity Benefit/Income Support recipients had no plans to (re)-enter employment and yet were leading productive and fulfilling lives.
- There is a need for explicit consideration of how to enable access to ill-health-related benefits designed to ameliorate risks of financial hardship.

Introduction

Given the low levels of employment among individuals with long-term health conditions, income replacement benefits (usually Incapacity Benefit [IB] or Income Support [IS] with a disability premium) play a crucial role in mitigating the economic impact of ill health. Moreover, benefits aimed at offsetting additional expenditure associated with illness and impairment (primarily Disability Living Allowance [DLA]) are an essential, if not necessarily fully adequate (Smith et al, 2004), contribution towards maintaining standards of living, including continued engagement with wider society (see Box 1 for a description of current benefits available).

However, recent government policy and public opinion highlights the large numbers of individuals receiving IB/IS and presents this situation as undesirable, often suggesting that many claimants should be in work and that their benefit receipt is unwarranted.[20] This view is being vigorously challenged (TUC, 2005) and clearly downplays existing evidence regarding the nature of the majority of IB/IS claimants, including the very low levels of fraud (Hedges and Sykes, 2001) and the complex obstacles to finding sustained employment (Ashworth et al, 2001; and see Chapter 4).

Furthermore, evidence indicates that take-up of benefits – that is, actual receipt – is often well below maximum, suggesting that significant numbers of people do not receive entitlement that could potentially improve their standard of living. For instance, the Disability Alliance suggests that take-up of DLA is just 40-60% of those eligible (Wayne, 2003). Bacon (2002) has shown that a large proportion of Jobseeker's Allowance claimants report ill health that restricts their ability to work, and other research identifies the slow rate at which jobseekers with health conditions move off unemployment-related benefits (Shaw et al, 1996; Smith et al, 2000) indicating that people do not necessarily take up ill-health-related benefits when they develop a health condition.

Box 1
SUMMARY INFORMATION REGARDING THE MAIN ILL-HEALTH-RELATED BENEFITS AVAILABLE TO WORKING-AGE ADULTS AT THE TIME OF THE STUDY IN THE UK

Incapacity Benefit (IB)

Eligibility criteria:
- Intended for people 'incapable of work because of sickness or disability'.
- Assessed as 'unable to perform own occupation' for first 28 weeks and thereafter as 'unfit for work'.
- Sufficient past National Insurance contributions.
- Only 'permitted work' is allowed – limited hours and earnings.

Weekly amount:
- Paid at three different rates (not including supplements that may be paid for dependants):
  1. Short-term IB lower rate: if do not get Statutory Sick Pay and sick for at least four days in a row, or qualify under rules for young people: £57.65.
  2. Short-term IB higher rate: paid if ill health for more than 28 weeks and less than 52 weeks: £68.20.
  3. Long-term IB: paid if ill health for over 52 weeks: £76.45.

Claiming process:
- Initially: self-completion of an application pack including Medical Certificate (sick note) from GP.
- After a period of receiving the benefit (around three months): self-completion of a questionnaire, the Personal Capability Assessment (PCA) (Part 1 relating to physical disabilities and Part 2 to mental disabilities). A score of 15 confirms eligibility for IB. Medical examination by a Department

---

[20] Interestingly, DLA is not given sustained attention in recent government policy documents.

for Work and Pensions (DWP) examining medical practitioner where a decision cannot be made on the basis of the PCA questionnaire.

- Fixed-term awards need to be renewed via a newly completed claim form, and this may also involve medical examination again.
- Ongoing claims assessed periodically and this may also involve a face-to-face medical examination.

Income Support (IS) (on grounds of ill health)

Eligibility criteria:
- Intended for people under 60 on a low income who are not working and not required to be seeking work (in this case those who are 'sick or disabled').
- Less than £8,000 savings. Dependent on partner's work and income.
- Insufficient National Insurance contributions to qualify for IB.

Weekly amount:
- Claimants receive a personal allowance plus premiums for 'disability', dependants and so on. Amounts vary with other household income. For example, single person allowance aged 25+ £55.65 plus disability premium £23.70.

Claiming process:
- As for IB, although forms are distinct.

Disability Living Allowance (DLA)

Eligibility criteria:
- Intended for people with 'severe physical or mental illness or disability'.
- Two components: mobility and care.
- Age (<65 years).
- Non-means-tested (not affected by savings or other income).
- Not affected by employment status.

Weekly amount:
- Paid at different rates depending on how the health condition affects the individual:
  - Care higher: £62.25; care middle: £41.65; care lower: £16.50.
  - Mobility higher: £43.45; mobility lower £16.50.
- Total ranges from £16.50 to £105.70

Claiming process:
- Self-completion of claim form detailing daily activities and capabilities. Claim form asks for permission to contact GP, but no certification from GP needs to be included.
- Medical examination by a DWP examining medical practitioner where a decision cannot be made on the basis of the questionnaire.
- Renewal of fixed-term awards, and periodic review as for IB.

Note: Various additional rules also apply, including some relating to UK residency. Recently planned changes to IB/IS rules are detailed in Appendix C.

The significant literature on benefit take-up in the UK has predominantly taken two forms. First, systematic comparisons of eligibility criteria with benefit receipt have been used to estimate take-up rates, primarily for means-tested benefits (for example, Falkingham, 1985; Fry and Stark, 1993; DWP, 2006a). These studies have not considered differentiation by ethnic group, despite a longstanding acknowledgement of the importance of such work (Craig, 1991). Second, a number of qualitative studies have explored factors influencing benefit take-up, including some that have examined the role of ethnicity (for example, Gordon and Newnham, 1985; NACAB, 1991; Law et al, 1994; Barnard and Pettigrew, 2003; Craig, 2004). This work provides some indication of the factors that may affect receipt of ill-health-related benefits across different ethnic groups, including those relating to both claimant behaviour and administrative response, which of course are interrelated (Platt, 2003).

It is clear that take-up of benefit increases with the amount of entitlement (DWP, 2006a; Pudney et al, 2004). This suggests that the perceived 'costs' of claiming in terms of time, effort, information needs, 'hassle' and stigma (Platt, 2003; Pudney et al, 2004) are weighed up against the potential monetary gains. Costs of claiming are unlikely to be constant across individuals and groups. Barnard and Pettigrew (2003) identified a range of potential barriers among older people from minority ethnic groups, including language issues, lack of a National Insurance number (among South Asian older women) and concerns about the impact of claiming on residence status. Fears of the system and the arduous nature of the claims process, while general issues, were enhanced for minority ethnic group members (see also Scharf et al, 2002).

Craig (2004) has drawn attention to the lack of adequate exploration of attitudes to claiming benefits among minority ethnic groups, and the available evidence suggests significant heterogeneity across groups and contexts. Molloy et al (2003) found that African, Caribbean and Pakistani respondents more commonly raised issues related to pride and avoidance of charity than White and Indian respondents. In contrast, Law et al (1994) found positive, rights-based attitudes to claiming among some Bangladeshi respondents alongside more resistant attitudes from others. In addition, an information deficit relating to both knowledge and familiarity with the 'system' is a significant issue for certain minority groups (Bloch, 1993; Scharf et al, 2002; Molloy et al 2003; Craig, 2004). Given the notoriously difficult claiming procedure for DLA, and a tightening of rules regarding eligibility for IB, such difficulties may be heightened for ill-health-related benefits.

Experience or anticipation of refusal, or requests for additional evidence, also increase costs of claiming (Gordon and Newnham, 1985; NACAB, 1996). Furthermore, the policy stance towards particular types of benefit (for example the recent focus on reducing claims for IB [DWP, 2006b]) or targeted at particular groups (for example the exclusion of asylum seekers from the mainstream benefits system [Bloch, 1997]) also shape the costs and benefits of claiming by presenting particular claims as undesirable or unwarranted. Those groups, therefore, that stand to gain the greatest proportional increase in income through the receipt of benefits may be the very same ones for whom the costs of claiming are high.

Moreover, it is also important to consider the possibility that those who claim may not be deemed eligible or awarded benefit. We know that in practice few claims for DLA are successful when not assisted by professional help; and in 2004 and 2005 fewer than half of new DLA claims resulted in an award (*Hansard*, 25 October 2005, Column 280W). Again, although information is limited, there is some evidence that minority ethnic groups are at a disadvantage (Bloch, 1997). This disadvantage is likely to be greater the higher the level of discretion within the system and the greater the scope for judgements to incorporate prejudicial assumptions or to allow particular emphasis on rules such as the much discussed 'habitual residence test' (Platt, 2003; House of Commons Work and Pensions Committee, 2005). In addition, differences in English language fluency and the extent to which assessment tools have cross-cultural validity may mean that certain minority ethnic groups are less likely to provide the 'right' answers and thus receive awards.

To date there has been little detailed investigation of the processes influencing people's experiences of claiming ill-health-related benefits. The present chapter brings together our qualitative and quantitative analyses to examine patterns of benefit take-up and the factors that influence access.

Patterns of benefit take-up[21]

Although current policy and public opinion might lead one to believe that both the decision to claim and the award of ill-health-related benefits is straightforward, our respondent narratives suggest otherwise. For many individuals the decision to submit a claim was not taken lightly, and the process of claiming was extremely stressful and time-consuming. As discussed in Chapter 4, many of our respondents continued working despite long-term health conditions. Furthermore, among those who were not working, some were not claiming any kind of state welfare benefit and others were receiving Job Seeker's Allowance.

In relation to DLA, both our quantitative and qualitative analyses indicated low levels of receipt. Table 3 shows the prevalence of DLA receipt calculated from our LFS analyses, and although it is not possible to calculate eligible non-receipt, the figures are suggestive of obstacles to claiming. Among all those reporting a long-term health condition, 12% reported receiving DLA, and this figure was 19% among those reporting limitations to daily activity. Ethnic group differences were also apparent. Multivariate analyses on the same data confirmed that, compared with White British respondents with comparable health and socioeconomic status, Pakistanis, Bangladeshis and Black Africans had much lower probabilities of receiving DLA.[22]

We were also able to produce some suggestive findings on levels and ethnic differentials in IB receipt. We considered receipt of IB among men only, since, given the National Insurance contributions requirements for eligibility, differences between women are much more likely to be complicated by differences in past economic activity rates. Moreover, IB incorporates dependants' allowances where eligible, so even those who themselves have a long-term health condition may, if their partner is receiving IB, receive support as a dependant, rather than separately.

Table 3: Prevalence of DLA receipt among working-age adults with long-term health condition and activity limitations by ethnic group

Ethnicity	% of respondents in receipt of DLA among those with:	
	a long-term health condition	an activity-limiting health condition
White British	12.4	19.2
Pakistani	11.9	15.7
Bangladeshi	7.5	10.2
Black African	9.5	15.8
Overall	12.2	18.9

Note: 'Overall' also includes other ethnic groups that were not the focus of our analyses.
Source: LFS, March 2002–February 2005, authors' analysis

---

[21] We do not report findings relating to Carer's Allowance here due to shortage of space and the fact that this benefit was rarely something that our respondents had considered. Nevertheless, where it was mentioned, similar issues emerged including: reluctance to claim; inadequacy of the benefit; complexities of the process; and rejection of claims.

[22] Logistic regression analyses were carried out on the probability of being in receipt of DLA among those with a long-term health condition, controlling for severity of condition, proxied by number of conditions and whether the condition was activity limiting. Controls for sex, age, educational qualifications, socioeconomic status, region and receipt of means-tested and other sickness-related benefits were also included. Standard errors were adjusted for repeat observations on individuals and coefficients with p-values of 0.05 or less were considered statistically significant. Full tables are available from the authors on request.

Figure 8 shows IB receipt among working-age men who were not currently working (but had worked in the past) with (a) a long-term health condition and (b) an activity-limiting long-term health condition. Unsurprisingly, rates of IB receipt were higher across all ethnic groups among those with an activity-limiting condition than those whose condition was not activity limiting. The figure also shows striking differences by ethnic group,[23] with the White British men having the highest proportions in receipt (around 55% of those with an activity-limiting condition) and the Bangladeshi men the lowest (just 27%).

Of course, we cannot reject the possibility that these different rates reflect different eligibility. One factor that may be relevant is recent migration to the UK and thus failure to accrue sufficient National Insurance contributions. As a check on this, we examined just those who either were born in the UK or immigrated more than five years ago. Although the 95% confidence intervals were wider, particularly for the Black African men, the basic pattern remained the same. Bangladeshi and Pakistani men were still significantly less likely than the White British men to receive IB (25% and 34% of those with an activity-limiting condition, compared with 55%).

While these results are not conclusive,[24] they do suggest greater obstacles to claiming among the minority ethnic groups, and this invites further investigation.

Figure 8: Proportion of men with a long-term health condition/activity-limiting long-term health condition in receipt of IB by ethnic group

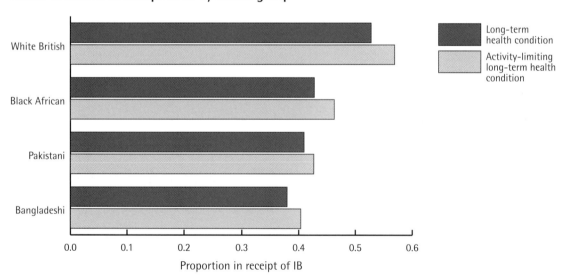

Notes: Proportions are based on data weighted by person weights. Standard errors were adjusted for repeat observations on individuals.
Source: LFS, pooled quarters, 2002-05

---

[23] Inspection of 95% confidence intervals confirmed no overlap between those for the White British majority and each of the minority ethnic groups.

[24] And a further issue in addition to eligibility is whether there is misidentification of benefits, in response to the questions.

Deciding to claim sickness benefits

We found significant commonalities across the four ethnic groups, suggesting that a complex of factors influences whether or not a claim is submitted for ill-health-related benefits, as we describe below. However, we also found evidence of ethnic differences in access.

Eligibility and legitimacy concerns

Perceptions of the legitimacy of claiming welfare benefits in general, and ill-health-related benefits in particular, importantly influenced whether or not a claim was made. Across all four ethnic groups many respondents expressed negative attitudes to the receipt of welfare benefits, referring to notions of 'scrounging', 'losing control', 'becoming lazy' and 'feeling degraded'. Such sentiments were particularly strongly expressed by our Ghanaian respondents.

> [Describing a period of ill health when out of work and unable to pay rent] 'No, no I didn't want to [seek benefit support]. Not that I have any pride in me, or that kind of thing. But with us Ghanaians, you don't feel happy about these things, you understand? You always want to work.' (Ghanaian man with long-term condition, 40-44 years)

> 'People say to me 'Why don't you go, why don't you pack your job in and, you know, get disability'. I don't want to do that. I like to work. I prefer to work. I've never been a sponger. For people like me. I mean, it's not quite like everybody's spongers, there's people, that's got disabilities and they can't work ... but the way I was brought up, that you worked, you didn't sponge off anybody. To claim [pause] is wrong.' (White English man with long-term condition, 55-59 years)

Of course, much of this discussion related to the situation where claiming benefits was placed in opposition to earning one's own income. However, it was also relevant where people were weighing up the pros and cons of seeking an ill-health-related benefit rather than an unemployment-related benefit (primarily Jobseeker's Allowance).

People's concerns around the illegitimacy and undesirability of claiming an ill-health-related benefit were closely related to the perceived negative implications of assuming the identity of 'incapacitated' (or 'unfit for work') or 'disabled' (as discussed in Chapter 3). In some cases, individuals refused to identify themselves as ill and/or disabled, in other cases individuals did consider themselves to be ill, but nevertheless did not feel 'ill enough' to warrant claiming an ill-health-related benefit, often comparing themselves to 'people out there who are more deserving'. In some cases, respondents expressed uncertainty and ambivalence regarding the 'right' course of action.

> 'I want to work. As to which benefit to be on [pause]. It's been going so long now I just feel guilty that I'm still [pause]. I'm being a sponger. When I was on it [IB] I did feel like I was perhaps swinging the lead a little bit, I wasn't really entitled to be on Incapacity Benefit. But since I've been really looking for work I realise no employer's going to take me on. So then, perhaps I am entitled to it!' (White English man with long-term condition, 40-45 years)

Concern about illegitimacy was a particular issue for several, although not all, respondents suffering from mental ill health.

[Talking about the fact that she has not yet considered claiming for IB] 'I don't think I could go to someone and say 'Oh god I can't work 'cos I suffer from anxiety or panic', you know? I don't know if I could go and tell people that. That would be very difficult.' (White English woman with long-term condition, 35-39 years)

Although DLA can be claimed regardless of employment status, this backdrop of required legitimacy (rather than eligibility per se) evidently also affected people's stance towards DLA. As noted in Chapter 3, many respondents were reluctant to assume a 'disabled' identity and this did appear to affect decisions to claim DLA. A common theme across all four ethnic groups was that of holding off claiming until really necessary.

'Disability, actually I haven't as yet, I am able to walk about to some extent ... and that's why I haven't applied, because I haven't become disabled as yet.' (Bangladeshi man with long-term condition, 45-49 years)

In addition, some respondents felt that taking DLA or IB would further solidify their identity as 'long-term ill' and 'disabled', and make a return to employment or active life less likely; something to be resisted at all costs.

'They were all pushing me to do that [take DLA]. I say 'I'm getting up. I will not stay in this bed like this'.... They said 'You stupid, you are mad'. But I said 'Look, all that I want, I want to be on my feet'.... Although things were hard. But, if I had compromised me, I'd feel it was a bit of compromising.... Because I don't want to be accommodated into that disability thing. Funnily enough, sometimes they [social workers] come here ... they will use 'disabled'. I say 'No, no, no, no! I'm not disabled!" (Ghanaian woman with long-term condition, 40-44 years)

[Talking about being declared 'fit for work' and having his IB entitlement stopped] 'There was also something rather nice about it 'cause I felt that I was healing, it was actually a sort of encouragement. It wouldn't be long till I'm actually working again.' (White English man with long-term condition, 40-44 years)

Notions of legitimacy were, however, flexible and also linked to perceptions of valued social roles. Claiming DLA was more acceptable for older individuals, mirroring the differential ideas about long-term health conditions by age discussed in Chapter 3. For Bangladeshi and Pakistani men, ill-health-induced economic inactivity appeared to be a relatively accepted role to assume even from age mid-forties onwards. Respondents talked of the high levels of un- and under-employment among younger, fitter men within their communities and the fact that available jobs were unsuitable for men of their age. These findings tend to support the argument that contextual factors (particularly a weak job market) can encourage individuals to present themselves as ill or incapacitated and therefore claim ill-health-related benefits rather than unemployment-related benefits (Fieldhouse and Hollywood, 1999; Beatty and Fothergill, 2005). However, it should be noted that not all Bangladeshi and Pakistani men who openly presented themselves as having a long-term health condition necessarily applied for ill-health-related benefits. Several were instead relying on family-level support and the quantitative findings presented above reveal that they were actually less likely than the White British group to be receiving ill-health-related benefits.

Notwithstanding the various disincentives mentioned above, our qualitative and quantitative findings on DLA receipt concurred with earlier work, in showing that the degree of financial hardship can play an important role in determining whether or not a claim for ill-health-related benefits is made. Our quantitative analysis showed that as occupational class decreased, the chances of receiving DLA increased. This may reflect differential 'need' for the benefit related in part to the chances of remaining in employment with a long-term health condition, as well as accumulated assets. The argument for economic incentives to claim DLA was also supported by the higher rates of receipt among those in receipt of IS compared with those not in receipt. That this is not purely a result of familiarity with the benefits system is indicated by the fact that people receiving unemployment benefits or National Insurance credits were *less* likely to receive DLA.

Our qualitative data also suggested that when faced with financial difficulty, individuals may ignore community proscriptions against claiming an ill-health-related benefit and actively seek out information on additional benefit entitlements, as in the case of several Ghanaian women who were single parents and the Pakistani woman who is quoted below.

> 'At that time we could not survive with the Income Support. I had some fights with him [husband] regarding this. I told him to get some more money somehow or other. He said he could not work. Then we consulted the doctor. He advised us to apply for Disability Allowance. Then we got help from this for our bills and insurance.' (Pakistani woman family member, 45-49 years)

It has been argued that the benefits system creates financial incentives for individuals to claim IB/IS rather than Jobseeker's Allowance (Beatty and Fothergill, 2005; DWP, 2006a). Some of our respondents did talk about the pros of receiving IB in terms of the higher amount received. However, the preference for IB was often not clear cut, for the reasons described above. Some also expressed the view that not having to look for work or participate in Job Centre activities was an advantage of being on IB, although these were individuals who perceived their health condition to be too severe for them to work and such activities as entirely frustrating.

> *Interviewer:* Would you prefer to be on Incapacity Benefit if possible?
>
> *Respondent:* If possible, yes.
>
> *Interviewer:* And why would you prefer to be on that?
>
> *Respondent:* Because I feel that, I feel more weak, more sick, that's why. And er, that's it. (Bangladeshi man with long-term condition, 50-54 years)

Social networks, access to information and 'know-how' about the system

Regardless of perceived need and legitimacy of claiming, individuals clearly have to be aware of available benefits and confident to engage with the system in order to make a successful claim for support. Across all the ethnic groups, some respondents expressed their feelings of ignorance and described difficulties encountered in accessing information regarding the benefits system and their entitlements. There was evidence that awareness of IB being a non-means-tested benefit was low.

> [Talking about his wife who is currently receiving Statutory Sick Pay] 'Honestly, that's how it works. If one of you is working, that's it, you get nothing. It's only if both of you are not working that you can start claiming. It's ridiculous, ridiculous. They penalise you for working in this country.' (White English man family member with own health condition, 60-64 years)

> [Talking about his wife who has diabetes and has stopped working] 'Well, I am employed. I cannot receive benefits as I work. Unless she is helped in her own right, and if you are aware of any help or advice you can give me then I will welcome it.' (Ghanaian man, family member, 50-54 years)

Awareness and understanding of DLA seemed particularly poor; many respondents had not heard of the benefit despite having had a long-term health condition for an extended period and, in some cases, receiving IB.

> 'We didn't know nothing about Disability Allowance or anything like that, ... I didn't know nothing about the system. [The social worker] goes 'Hasn't the Income Support, the social services ever interviewed you or asked your mum about this, 'cause she's got that mental illness?', and I said 'No, I didn't know nothing'. She goes 'You've lost years and years of her Disability Allowance!'' (Pakistani woman, family member, 30-34 years)

Those who had heard of DLA often held misconceptions about eligibility criteria, for instance thinking that the benefit is means-tested and therefore that working or having a working spouse would mean ineligibility; believing that DLA cannot be claimed simultaneously with IB; or, in contrast, that IB receipt is a requirement for DLA eligibility; and for several Bangladeshi and Pakistani respondents that DLA is only intended for individuals with severe physical or mental impairments and not incapacity associated with chronic illness.

Poor knowledge was compounded by a common perception among all ethnic groups that the benefits system was complicated and stressful. Many respondents specifically talked about the onerous task of completing the long forms and, in relation to DLA, this undoubtedly put many people off submitting a claim for the benefit. Several respondents talked about gradually learning how to negotiate and battle their way through the system. Although felt across the board, respondents with lower levels of education or English language competency clearly found this a particular obstacle.

The multivariate quantitative analyses of probability of DLA receipt among those with a long-term health condition revealed a complex picture of the association between educational level and receipt. Overall, qualifications were associated with lower receipt, even when severity of the condition and occupational class were controlled for. This was surprising. The raw data, however, indicated that this pattern, whereby education 'doesn't help' might not hold across all the ethnic groups. Further multivariate analysis suggested that White British and Pakistani respondents were more likely to be in receipt of DLA at lower compared with higher levels of qualifications. However, the pattern was reversed for Bangladeshis and Black Africans, with higher levels of qualifications meaning higher receipt compared both with those of the same ethnic group with lower qualifications and to White British and Pakistani respondents with the same level of qualifications. Small cell sizes and overlapping confidence intervals make these conclusions tentative. They are, however, consistent with our qualitative findings.

A heavy reliance on personal social networks and word of mouth for information and 'know-how' about benefits was evident for Pakistani, Bangladeshi and White English respondents. Many respondents mentioned friends as the ones who had initially introduced the possibility of claiming an ill-health-related benefit. However, despite this apparent similarity across these ethnic groups, the domination of social networks by ties within the same ethnic group resulted in ethnic variation in the availability of information. The Pakistani local networks stood out as being particularly well informed of the benefit system and there was evidence of active sharing of information between Pakistani individuals.

> 'I have helped three to four people, those who come to [name of group], they weren't getting disability, so I told them this is the way, I got them the form from the social service, in a legal way, like 'here, here is the department', ... I used to take them.' (Pakistani man, family member, 50-54 years)

In contrast, the Bangladeshi networks were less productive and respondents less well informed of available options. Importantly, however, many respondents in both the Pakistani and Bangladeshi groups expressed feelings of alienation and exclusion from 'mainstream' society and services, factors that reinforced their tendency to rely on 'our own people', despite the variable ability of this strategy to meet needs.

> [In answer to a question about whether receiving support from charities or organisations] 'I am searching for such groups, really I want to know how these other organisations work, but I have not been able to find out much. I got a leaflet, but where they are located and what they do I have not been able to find out. I have asked friends or people that I know. I try to find out if there are any Bengali people among them, who could help, but I have not been able to find anybody.' (Bangladeshi man, family member, 40-44 years)

Interestingly, among the Ghanaians, a more complex picture emerged, reflecting the diverse linguistic, cultural, religious and socioeconomic profile of this group. Among those who were better educated and longer established, many had directly sought information from 'mainstream' services, including the Job Centre. The heightened concealment of ill health within this community (see Chapter 3), combined with a similar sensitivity regarding the discussion of financial matters, appeared to discourage exchange of information on receipt of benefits, and consequently means that social networks are less productive on this topic. Furthermore, although the broader identity of 'Ghanaian' was clearly meaningful to individuals in certain circumstances, a variety of sub-networks of association and resource exchange (often based on clan heritage or 'home town' affiliation) were more relevant in many cases, and acted to both include and exclude people. More recent Ghanaian migrants with poorer English language skills and less confidence in dealing with the 'system' appear to suffer as a result, finding it difficult to access information and advice.

Experiences of the claiming process: battling with the system

Given the complexity of the claiming process, particularly for DLA, over and above awareness of the benefit, access to specialist support is important if a claim is to have a high chance of success. Almost across the board, whether respondents' claims had been successful or not, they described the process of claiming ill-health-related benefits as complex, stressful and time-consuming. Many felt that the system does not trust people, is inequitable and unpredictable and that benefits are very difficult to get.

> 'I am a support worker and I'd say I fill in around four to five of these DLA forms a week. And you know, I never know when I send them off which ones are going to be successful.' (Pakistani woman, advice worker, 35-39 years, group discussion, Phase Three)

> [Recounting his experience of an unsuccessful appeal for IB before committee] 'When I came out I laughed. They said 'Why did you laugh?' I said 'I laughed because I should have come here with a bag of lies then I could win the appeal. I told you the truth, this is why I lost the appeal. I know lots of people, they are not very sick … I had radiation, I had major surgery, I am asthmatic, I have got so much problem and you are saying that I am fit' That's why I laughed.' (Bangladeshi man, with long-term condition, 35-39 years)

Our qualitative work revealed that few individuals from any of the ethnic groups had received specialist support in claiming ill-health-related benefits. This is perhaps surprising for the Bangladeshi and Pakistani respondents given the relatively large numbers of community-based organisations offering benefits advice and catering specifically to the needs of these individuals. The picture is less surprising for Ghanaians, since there were few support organisations for this group. Furthermore, there was evidence that where such support had been offered on an ad-hoc basis, take-up was extremely low, again reflecting the aversion to discussing financial matters and the lack of information exchange on this topic within Ghanaian networks. Interestingly, many of our White English respondents expressed feelings of being poorly supported in comparison with minority ethnic groups who were perceived to receive tailor-made services and additional support. A lack of specialist support to claims is clearly an issue affecting all ethnic groups. However, lower levels of education, poor English language competency and lack of experience with state bureaucracy are likely to make this a particularly serious problem for significant numbers among the minority ethnic groups.

Importantly, several individuals suffering from mental ill health cited the benefits system as a major factor contributing stress to their lives and further undermining their health. For a number of individuals, problems gaining access to benefits were compounded by other bureaucratic and financial difficulties including being in arrears with rent or loan repayments, or struggling to secure housing adaptations or a housing transfer. Delays in the processing of claims were commonly reported and had significant financial implications for those with no other source of income. Moving from Statutory Sick Pay or unemployment without payment to IB/IS had been particularly difficult for several respondents.

Respondents also often felt at the mercy of other individuals, particularly their GPs, since they were required to provide sickness certification[25] along with claim forms. Although experiences were very mixed, several respondents had had extreme difficulty in getting their GP to provide sickness certification and many more reported that their GP had been reluctant at times to provide a sick note. Furthermore, our evidence suggests that the Bangladeshi community in Tower Hamlets faced particular problems in this respect, and that resistance to providing sickness certification was racialised in some cases.

> [Recounting the story of her seven-month wait for diagnosis with disc prolapse and sickness certification] 'Going to the GP was also no better. They would say 'You have back pain' and that's it. They were not interested in listening to me any further. At that time the GP's behaviour towards me was very bad. I had to go to them for my sick note, because I was working. Every time I went up to the GP for my sick note they would tell me off, using abusive language like 'You Asian, Bengali people always prefer to live off benefits, and do not like to work'. I would say half my worries are because of my doctor.' (Bangladeshi woman with long-term condition, 35-39 years)

Many of our respondents had been through the process of having their fitness for work (or eligibility for DLA) assessed by a DWP medical assessor. However, very few had much idea of how the assessor actually made their assessment and many expressed distrust or lack of confidence in the process. In a number of cases, a desire to 'perform well', an important component of self-identity, was at odds with the need to demonstrate 'incapacity', so that individuals inadvertently undermined their claim.

A large number of respondents had had the experience of having a claim for DLA or IB/IS rejected, or their entitlement taken away or reduced some time after their original claim. Individuals who were currently in receipt also often expressed uncertainty as to whether their benefit would be withdrawn in the future and thus a feeling of vulnerability. While some respondents took rejection in their stride, others found the process extremely

---

[25] 'Sickness certification' is the term used by the DWP to refer to the process whereby a GP gives an assessment regarding their patient's ability to work relating to incapacity arising from disease or impairment.

stressful, receiving the decision as a negation of their own suffering. A number of respondents had experienced the particularly stressful situation where a DWP medical assessor had pronounced them 'fit for work' and yet they had been laid off work by their employers on the grounds of ill health, or considered unfit for work by benefits agency staff.

> 'Oh you're not fit for work therefore you're not entitled to JSA [Jobseeker's Allowance]. And then you're not disabled enough to be on Incapacity Benefit. You get bounced between the two. My claim's been stopped a few times.' (White English man with long-term condition, 40-44 years)

In several cases, respondents felt that mental health conditions and their associated impairments were not appropriately assessed.

> 'They were thinking she's getting better, she's getting better, but they were just looking at her mobility. And they weren't looking at her state of mind, and that's why they have cancelled all that, and just give her, not even £15.' (Pakistani woman, family member, 30-34 years)

Other factors that individuals felt were not adequately taken into account in the process of declaring an individual 'fit for work' included the burden of health appointments; the combined impact of multiple health conditions; the unpredictability of symptoms; the significance of pain and fatigue; and an individual's capabilities in relation to the type of work they would normally do (for example heavy manual labour) or the type of work that is available given their qualifications.

Across all four ethnic groups there was a variety of responses to a rejected claim. While some respondents had confidently appealed against the decision, for others the rejection had undermined their confidence in the legitimacy of their claim, or their energy to face the stress of appealing. For some, rejection had even discouraged them from seeking other benefits and support. Again, there were few cases where specialist support had been accessed in preparing an appeal. Poor English language skills and lack of confidence in dealing with the system (in some cases compounded by past stressful experiences) tended to exacerbate these obstacles for significant numbers of the Bangladeshi, Pakistani and Ghanaian respondents.

> 'When I was ill and unable to move my friends told me that I should claim Disability Allowance. But I did ask for it and I was turned down. There are other things my friend tells me that I can claim. Some money for home repairs and things like that. That I haven't. And there are other things that I do not know about. To be honest, I am just not interested to get into this, because I am never lucky, and I do not want unnecessary hassle.' (Bangladeshi woman with long-term condition, 35-39 years)

Implications of receiving ill-health-related benefits

Chapter 4 noted the complexity of the 'work versus benefits calculation' that many individuals may make. Here we are concerned more directly with the implications of receiving ill-health-related benefits themselves. It is increasingly argued that being in receipt of IB/IS leads to marginalisation and exclusion from employment opportunities even when labour market conditions are favourable (Beatty and Fothergill, 2005; DWP, 2006a).

Our qualitative work tended to reveal a more complex picture. It was certainly true that some respondents who were receiving benefits felt outside the mainstream of society and expressed strong preferences for (re-)entering the world of work. However, only very few specifically regarded receiving IB/IS as a factor that discouraged employment and this seemed to relate more to the potential undermining of self-identity than to exclusion from DWP support services (which many found inadequate, see Chapter 4).

Furthermore, we found evidence that for some individuals with long-term health conditions, being labelled as 'fit for work' and therefore receiving Jobseeker's Allowance, rather than IB/IS, was a factor that exacerbated their feelings of marginalisation and frustration precisely because their health condition, symptoms and specialist needs were not acknowledged by the system.

A further category of cases were individuals who saw IB/IS as an appropriate and temporary support to allow time to recover their health. Such individuals had often taken steps independently (or with support from non-DWP agencies), when they felt the time was right, to re-engage with the labour market despite their not having to attend regular meetings at the Job Centre.

It is also important to document the cases where individuals were in receipt of IB/IS, had no plans to (re)-enter the labour market, but could nevertheless be considered to be leading productive and fulfilling lives, including some who were active volunteers and others who took important caring or domestic roles within their families. In short, we did not find strong evidence for a negative effect of receiving IB/IS in and of itself.

> 'Thereafter I never went back to work and I am not physically fit to get to work. The doctors as well have to tick me off as being physically fit to get back to work and they don't think I am physically fit and I don't consider myself to be physically fit. At present I don't have a job and I live with my daughter on Income Support and I am happy that way.' (Bangladeshi woman with long-term condition, 35-39 years)

Since DLA is not an income-replacement benefit, but rather is intended to offset additional expenditure associated with illness, it is of interest to examine the ways in which DLA was used. For those respondents who received DLA, even if at the lowest rate, currently £16 per week, it did seem to make a significant difference to their quality of life, reflecting the fact that those who claim tend to be poorer than those who do not bother. Likewise, withdrawal of the benefit can have a significant impact. A White English woman aged 55-59 years explained to us that when her DLA payments were stopped she had to get rid of her telephone. She simply could not pay the bills. She described how she now has problems making contact with her doctor, frequently misses appointments and relies on her daughter, who lives several miles away, to liaise with the GP and hospital staff on her behalf. In effect, receiving DLA had enabled her to maintain more effective social contact – very significant for someone who has trouble walking and travelling beyond the home.

The way in which DLA payments were used within the household varied. In some cases this money was simply contributed to a 'common pot'. However, several recipients identified specific items of expenditure to which this money was directed and in most cases this related to mobility. That said, many felt that the payments were insufficient to offset the increased transport costs that they faced, particularly those associated with hospital visits.

Berthoud (2006) calculated that just 9% of DLA recipients were in work, and found that among recipients those with less severe conditions were no more likely to be working than those with more severe conditions, suggesting that it plays a negligible role in facilitating employment. Our qualitative analyses suggest that this is in part because individuals tend only to claim if their health condition and associated impairments are serious and also due to lack of awareness that DLA can be used to support individuals into work (among some assessors within the benefits system as well as the general population).

Importantly, however, DLA money may contribute to an individual's participation in and connection with the social world around them in the other ways. Making visits to relatives and buying gifts were important ways that DLA payments could facilitate individuals' investments in reciprocal social networks (a theme we take up in Chapter 6).

Conclusions

Both our quantitative and qualitative data suggest significant barriers to claiming ill-health-related benefits and also suggest greater obstacles to claiming among our minority ethnic groups of focus. Among our qualitative respondents, low levels of uptake appeared to be in part related to negative attitudes towards revealing ill health and concerns about the legitimacy of claiming benefits, patterns that were particularly evident among the Ghanaians, and which appear to be reinforced by current government policy and associated public opinion. However, limited access to information and specialist support to negotiate the complex system appeared to be much more significant obstacles, and ones that were heightened for many of the minority ethnic individuals. Ethnically dominated social networks resulted in differential access to information and 'know-how'. Clearly, government and voluntary agencies have a responsibility to ensure that services are accessible and appropriate to the needs of marginalised groups.

The qualitative work also revealed how access to information and personal examples of successful claimants can break down perceived barriers to claiming as in the case of our Pakistani community where we came across clusters of individuals who were all receiving DLA. Although not all individuals with long-term health conditions are eligible to claim ill-health-related benefits, and some actively decide that they prefer not to, our findings nevertheless suggest that significant numbers of individuals are discouraged from pursuing claims for support even when living on extremely low incomes. Such findings clearly imply a need for explicit consideration of how to enable, rather than merely restrict (as current policy documents emphasise), access to benefits designed to support those unable to work through ill health and to ameliorate some of the consequent risks of hardship for them and their families.

6

Long-term health conditions and social participation

SUMMARY POINTS

- Lack of social participation is both a dimension of poverty in and of itself and may also undermine access to other important resources.
- Most respondents identified maintaining social contact and accessing social support as major concerns since the onset of ill health.
- Most respondents socialised primarily within their ethnic group, and the four groups showed some distinctive patterns in types of informal and formal social activity. Bangladeshi and Pakistani networks carried particular reciprocal obligations.
- Bangladeshi, Pakistani and particularly Ghanaian women were more constrained in their social contact than White English women or men from their communities. Quantitative analyses suggested that such differences were only partly explained by low income.
- Quantitative analyses indicated that for men caring was associated with lower social participation, but that ill health was not. For women, ill health was linked to lower social participation, but caring was not.
- Qualitative analysis found that many men and women felt that both caring and ill health had substantial impacts on social life. Many individuals *experienced* social participation less positively in the face of ill health, often because social ties did not provide valued support. Social networks were often a burden for Bangladeshi and Pakistani women.
- A complex of factors made securing social support from informal networks difficult including: reluctance to seek help; fear of using up favours; the need to reciprocate; mistrust; and feelings of vulnerability.
- Formal groups and organisations were often no better at providing valued practical and material assistance. Many individuals were reluctant to join ill-health-specific groups, particularly when the perceived focus on talking about ill health was not felt to be useful.
- Individuals with higher income appeared better able to maintain social participation and to secure the types of social support that they need.
- Black Africans (and Ghanaians in the qualitative work) had particularly high risks of social isolation.

Introduction

In seeking to understand the links between long-term ill health and poverty, a focus on social participation is warranted for two interrelated reasons.[26] First, low social participation

---

[26] In addition, social networks may themselves provide a direct, protective effect in relation to ill health. A large number of epidemiological studies have found positive associations between measures of social networks and social support and mortality (for example, Vogt et al, 1992; Eng et al, 2002; Berkman et al, 2004). Related work in the field of social psychology has documented the benefits of social support to individual well-being, self-reported health and adjustment to living with health conditions (for example, Sherbourne et al, 1992; Holahan et al, 1995). These issues relate more closely to our discussion of 'resilience' in Chapter 3.

can be considered a dimension of poverty (Townsend, 1979). In 1999, a study of poverty and social exclusion found that 80% of the British population thought that visits to friends and family were necessary and nearly two thirds (64%) considered that the ability to have friends or family round for a meal was a necessity (Gordon et al, 2000). Social and leisure activities were also stressed in the material deprivation measures incorporated into the government's child poverty targets (DWP, 2003b), and lack of social support can be considered an aspect of 'social exclusion' (Burchardt, 2000b). It is therefore of empirical interest to investigate the extent to which those with long-term health conditions are more susceptible to such deprivation. There is some evidence that ill health itself is associated with declining social networks (Courtens et al, 1996) as it undermines people's ability (and inclination) to invest in and maintain their social ties (Charmaz, 2000), however the evidence on the relationship between social participation and ill health is not extensive.

Second, social networks and resources are potentially instrumental. A range of studies has illustrated the ways in which social networks provide opportunities and access to other types of resources, such as job opportunities and informal loans (Montgomery, 1991; Wood and Salway, 2000; Basu and Altinay, 2003), resources that may help to reduce the impact of long-term ill health on living standards. Furthermore, a growing literature documents the ways in which 'social capital' may be linked to better health outcomes at individual and community level[27] (see Cooper et al, 1999; Hawe and Sheill, 2000). Social networks may therefore play a 'buffering role' in the face of stress or ill health (Whelan, 1993). However, it has been noted that it is important to distinguish between the range and frequency of contact within networks and the actual quality or nature of support provided through such social ties (McLeod et al, 2006).

Some individuals with long-term health conditions actively seek to establish new social networks with individuals facing similar circumstances, for instance via 'self-help' groups. Indeed, the assertion that such social contact can be beneficial is one premise that underpins the recent expansion of lay-led self-management programmes. However, the tendency to join such support networks varies by type of condition and personal circumstances (Davidson et al, 2000).

Whether and how ethnicity affects social participation and its links to long-term ill health has received relatively little attention to date. There is also limited understanding of the ways in which interventions by statutory or voluntary services might effectively provide the types of social support needed by individuals and families living with long-term conditions (Kawachi and Berkman, 2001).

Social participation: networks and activities

Our qualitative work revealed that, irrespective of health status, the extent of social networks and patterns of social participation varied greatly between individuals and families. Notwithstanding this general diversity, important variations along the lines of gender, ethnicity and generation were evident. Importantly, much social participation occurred within ethnic groups, and for many of the minority ethnic respondents this was felt to be normal and appropriate.

---

[27] However, the hugely varied use of the term 'social capital', particularly its dual use both as a description of individual or family access to social resources and as a characteristic of communities as a whole, is unhelpful. We opt here for a focus on the networks and resources that are available to individuals, although we do highlight the ways in which these are influenced by membership of particular ethnic and geographical communities (see also Chapter 2).

Informal social activities

Considering first 'informal' socialising, the four ethnic communities tended to have distinct patterns. Social networks for White English respondents were often centred on pubs, cafés or informal groups such as those meeting regularly to play bingo in community centres. Although information exchange and assistance did clearly take place at times, these networks were primarily perceived by respondents as sources of entertainment and leisure. Socialising within the home was uncommon, and often did not extend beyond close friends sharing a cup of tea. Some gendered patterns were evident. For instance, women were more likely to socialise through their children, and men were more likely to go to pubs alone with the expectation of meeting familiar faces. Some social activities were also dominated by one sex or the other, for instance bingo was a female-dominated activity. However, social spaces were not gendered to the same extent as for the Bangladeshi and Pakistani communities.

Among the Bangladeshi and Pakistani respondents, family networks were more commonly mentioned than among the White English respondents. In these two groups, visiting and eating in each others' homes was common. While this primarily involved the extended family, it could also include friends, colleagues and even acquaintances. Importantly, such social participation was often discussed in terms of obligation and expectation and was not associated with simple enjoyment.

Social participation was particularly tied to the home for many Bangladeshi and Pakistani women, for whom expectations of appropriate female behaviour may imply restricted interaction in public spaces. Some of our Bangladeshi and Pakistani female respondents felt constrained by these expectations and highlighted difficulties in accessing other forms of social participation.

> 'So I've not um, socialised for some reason.... Because I wasn't allowed to socialise when I was living with my in-laws, erm, it just became a habit of not socialising.... It was wrong then and it's wrong now.' (Pakistani woman with long-term condition, 30-34 years)

However, some Pakistani and Bangladeshi women had found ways to circumvent such restrictions by initiating their own female social gatherings, often religion based, at home in the absence of husbands and presenting these as legitimate activities.

Informal social networks for our Ghanaian respondents often involved visiting each other's houses for prayers and parties, as well as gatherings in community centres. For a large number of respondents who identified themselves as 'Ashanti' (having origins in the Ashanti/Asante region of Ghana) attending funeral celebrations was one of the most important ways of socialising and maintaining networks. The church was also an important source of friendships. Much socialising was again family based, particularly among the middle-aged and older people, and this meant that for many single individuals social interaction was largely restricted to church-going. Further, the Ghanaian community was more geographically spread across London than our other minority ethnic communities. As one female, single, Ghanaian respondent with a long-term health condition, aged 40-44 years, said, 'My social life is only going to church. I don't have any social life. Because you go out with somebody and … I don't see myself going out alone.' The heavy demands of work (see Chapter 4) put further constraints on many Ghanaians' opportunities for socialising.

Across all four communities some respondents, particularly older people, felt that ideal patterns of socialising were currently compromised by factors beyond individual control. White English people talked of loss of family networks and closure of pubs; while first generation minority ethnic respondents compared fast-paced and individualistic UK life with the way they used to socialise 'back home': 'Everybody is busy ... you know, people have no time, you know, for one another, they have the ..., you know, the system back home, people coming and visit' (Pakistani man, family member, 55-59 years).

Formal social activities

We also found some distinctive patterns across the ethnic groups in patterns of engagement with 'formal' groups and organisations. Among Ghanaians, membership and participation in organised groups was, for many, a central part of their social lives. Individuals were often members of several organisations and attended regular meetings and events. A plethora of organisations, often based on shared town of origin, old school or college, or professional association, existed, and these were commonly mixed-sex associations. For members, these organisations offered a sense of belonging and leisure activities were frequently complemented by supportive functions.

Among our Pakistani and Bangladeshi communities, group or organisation membership was less of an integral part of social participation than for the Ghanaians. However, group formation on the basis of shared ethnicity was a meaningful concept for many. Social spaces where individuals could come together with others who shared their language and 'culture', as well as gender and life-cycle stage, were valued, particularly by older individuals who were outside the labour market or no longer preoccupied with household responsibilities. Importantly, some groups that had originally been established primarily to provide companionship also offered valuable opportunities for exchange of information and advice. In addition, training classes in both localities provided by community-based organisations often evolved into ethnically specific groups and provided an environment for people, particularly women, to meet socially.

Among our White English respondents, group membership on the basis of ethnicity was not meaningful, nor was being a member of groups or organisations an expected part of social life. Group membership was much more a matter of individual interest, and many individuals engaged in no group activities at all. As one respondent (man with a long-term condition, 40-44 years) put it: 'I'm not a joiner'.

The patterns of social participation suggested by our qualitative work were largely represented at the aggregate level in the Home Office Citizenship Survey (HOCS) data. The HOCS asked people about four dimensions of social participation: (i) having friends or family round to the home, (ii) going out to friends' or family members' homes; (iii) going out, and (iv) being involved in a club or organised activity. Table 4 illustrates that Black Africans showed a greater tendency towards organised activities, especially among women; and Pakistanis and Bangladeshis showed much stronger patterns of reciprocal visiting.

The impacts of long-term health conditions on social participation

Interviews with respondents and family members revealed that many felt that their social lives had undergone thorough change since the onset of ill health. The comment 'I don't have a social life' was very common and was heard from respondents across all four ethnic groups. The vast majority of respondents valued social contact beyond their immediate family and saw the effects of ill health on social participation as impacting importantly upon their quality of life. In addition, for some, 'being sociable' was a major part of self-identity and the loss of this element of their lives was therefore felt particularly severely.

Exploring the basic patterns of social participation across the four dimensions in the HOCS among those with a long-term health condition suggested that ill health restricts

Table 4: Percentage engaging in different forms of social activity among those of working age (18–59/64) by ethnic group and sex

	Has friends or family round once a fortnight or more often	Goes round to friends or family once a fortnight or more often	Goes out once a fortnight or more often	Is involved with a club or some organised activity once a month or more often
Men				
White British	63	59	71	54
Pakistani	68	66	55	52
Bangladeshi	77	69	57	51
Black African	61	50	56	58
All men	63	59	70	54
Women				
White British	66	64	64	53
Pakistani	72	62	45	36
Bangladeshi	71	70	44	32
Black African	55	46	44	60
All women	65	63	64	52

Note: Percentages are based on weighted counts; unweighted counts 5,403 (men), 6,307 (women).
Source: 2001 HOCS

social activity across the groups, particularly (and unsurprisingly) in relation to going out (comparing Table 4 with Table 5). The effect seemed to be especially strong for minority ethnic women in this respect; and involvement in clubs was also reduced for Black

Table 5: Percentage of those with a long-term health condition engaging in different forms of social activity among those of working age (18–59/64) by ethnic group and sex

	Has friends or family round once a fortnight or more often	Goes round to friends or family once a fortnight or more often	Goes out once a fortnight or more often	Is involved with a club or some organised activity once a month or more often
Men				
White British	60	49	62	50
Pakistani	62	53	29	46
Bangladeshi	66	54	35	42
Black African	63	43	28	46
All men with a long-term health condition	59	50	60	51
Women				
White British	64	59	53	46
Pakistani	57	47	27	24
Bangladeshi	70	80	16	14
Black African	46	32	34	35
All women with a long-term health condition	63	58	52	46

Note: Percentages are based on weighted counts; unweighted counts = 5,403 (men), 6,307 (women).
Source: 2001 HOCS

Africans with a long-term health condition. Overall, the results are broadly consistent with the qualitative findings. The results for carers were more diverse and, based on small samples, were not straightforward to interpret.

However, within the qualitative work, closer inspection suggested that in some cases respondents were better connected and took part in more social networks than their descriptions of loss would imply. Nevertheless, in such cases the *experience* of social participation seems to have become qualitatively different. For example, one White English respondent continued to participate fully, but her experience of depression meant that such participation had ceased to be a source of pleasure. Similarly, a Bangladeshi respondent managed to maintain her provision of hospitality, despite ill health, but found entertaining guests to be a huge burden and felt the expectations on her as an imposition.

The importance of reciprocal networks often means that the maintenance of social contact comes at a cost and may add to the burdens of ill health or caring even as it keeps individuals and families connected to wider community. Ill health (or the experience of living/caring for someone who has a long-term condition) therefore appears to affect the ways in which people experience 'normal' participation and the extent to which their social networks fulfil their most pressing needs. This should be borne in mind when considering the findings on patterns of contact and the impact of ill health from the quantitative data below.

Reasons for changes in social participation

A range of physical, psychological, financial and social factors were identified in the qualitative interviews as constraints on the ability to participate. Respondents from the different ethnic groups tended to focus on the effect of ill health on different dimensions of social life, reflecting the somewhat diverse 'typical' patterns described above. Several respondents felt that the actual physical limitations posed by their condition, particularly mobility problems and reduced energy, made it difficult for them to socialise. Not being able to maintain a presentable house to entertain people at home because ill health made housework difficult had a major effect on some female Bangladeshi and Pakistani respondents' ability to maintain social contacts. Although White English respondents also expressed concerns about the upkeep of their houses, since entertaining at home was a less integral part of their social lives its impact on social participation was less keenly felt. Instead, White English respondents felt that not being able to go to the pub and bingo, drink or play sport constrained their social lives.

Further, some White English respondents felt that not being able to go to work had a major impact on their social life. Similarly, some Ghanaian respondents felt that not being able to go to parties and funerals restricted their social networks and ability to maintain them. A large number of respondents from all ethnic groups felt worried and preoccupied about their condition, which left little energy for maintaining social contacts. Some respondents described a lack of confidence in building new networks because of their home-centred existence.

> 'Nothing happens, when you sort of sit about nothing happens to you so if you go out to these people you've got nothing to talk about. I suppose now all I want is to watch *Eastenders*.' (White English man with long-term condition, 60-64 years)

Similarly, a fear of stigma due to ill health, especially where the symptoms were felt to have affected physical appearance, was another reason for avoiding social contacts, and there was some evidence that this was more of a concern among minority ethnic respondents.

'English people don't ask you this question. White people look at you and realise, probably he had an accident. That's why they don't ask you a question. Single White person did not ask me. Our people, they stop me and ask me what happened. Bengali people, they ask, what happened, your body is spoilt, you used to look so handsome. Like that they make you crazy.' (Bangladeshi man with long-term condition, 35-39 years)

Many of those with long-term conditions relied on other family members for help in going out, which was another significant constraint. Importantly, although some respondents were disappointed with friends or family in terms of the help they received in maintaining social contact, very few expressed more general feelings of society letting them down or creating obstacles for them to participate socially (aside from the concerns regarding people's negative reactions discussed above and in Chapter 3). This was consistent with the general lack of identification with the 'social model' of disability among our respondents (see Chapter 7 for potential policy and practice implications).

Our qualitative work suggested that the impact of ill health on social participation is mediated by the interplay of other resources, particularly family structure, employment and education. Married respondents with children had more options to socialise vicariously through their family members, especially through their spouses as compared with those living on their own. There was some evidence to suggest that wives were more active than husbands in maintaining social networks so that men with long-term conditions might not become as isolated as women in similar circumstances. For example, a Bangladeshi respondent whose physical appearance had been affected by illness was reluctant to go out to socialise, but was able to maintain social contacts through his wife who made arrangements for close friends and relatives to visit them at home. In some cases children also open up access to networks through their parents, especially for mothers. Similarly, several respondents in secure jobs were able to maintain good social lives despite their ill health because of access to a wide range of contacts through work, their ability to reciprocate in many different ways such as providing advice and information and their better financial situation, which allowed them to alter their patterns of socialising. For instance, one White English woman in secure employment described how, since being more disabled, she avoids going to noisy pubs but enjoys quiet meals out with her friends.

Relative impact of different factors on social participation

In order to explore the impact of ill health and caring on social participation further, we returned to the HOCS and constructed a measure of participation in terms of the likelihood of *not* participating, by combining the four measures of participation into a single scale (0 to 4) and using multivariate analysis.[28]

Looking first at men, before taking income into account, lack of social participation was associated with increasing age. Having a partner and a child under five were also associated with less participation. A partner in themselves might be considered a form of social contact, as discussed above, substituting for or enabling other forms of social activity; and a young child would be expected to reduce options for going out. The biggest influence on lack of social participation was educational qualifications, with low participation less likely as qualifications increased. This was over and above employment status, so it was not explained by the greater chance of being in work and thus having work-based contacts, which were shown to have a role in our qualitative data. Indeed,

---

[28] We carried out separate ordered probit regressions for men and women to assess the effect of various factors, including ethnicity, ill health and caring responsibilities, on levels of social participation according to this scale and controlling for age, partnership, qualifications, presence of children and employment status. Tables of the models are available from the authors on request.

other research suggests that the role of employment in preventing forms of social exclusion is at best ambiguous and at worst negative (Bailey, 2006; Levitas, 2006). Higher qualifications are associated with higher income, considered further below, thus making more opportunities affordable, but they are also associated with a more diverse range of social contacts and activities.

Once these variables were held constant, the only ethnic group to show a statistically significant difference from the White British majority were the Black Africans, who had increased risks of low social participation. This accords with the qualitative findings of the greater difficulty in sustaining networks at longer distances among our sample of Ghanaians, the heavy pressures of work, and the greater sense of isolation that they expressed.

Caring was found to increase the risks of low participation among men, consistent with the responses from the small number of male carers within our qualitative sample. However, having a health condition had no significant impact on non-participation in our quantitative analyses. This is surprising in light of the qualitative work, which suggested that respondents experienced a variety of constraints due to ill health. This discrepancy could be explained in part by the fact that our qualitative work was conducted in a highly deprived area and the sample characteristics therefore differ from those in the national survey data, although further statistical exploration did not support this explanation.[29] Instead, the observation in our qualitative work that the meaning of social activity can change in the light of ill health seems important – simply *engaging* in activity does not necessarily imply a positive experience or health-related benefits.

Our quantitative analyses provided no evidence to suggest that the effects of ill health on social participation among men varied with ethnicity for any of the ethnic groups considered, which was consistent with the qualitative work.[30]

A problem that could be raised in relation to our analysis is that our indicator of participation does not actually measure frequency of contact. Within any one form of participation, a high level of activity beyond the threshold could substitute for other forms of activity. For example, an individual could be having so many visitors as to preclude going out – their score in terms of lack of participation would then be fairly high – but they would nevertheless be experiencing a great deal of social activity.

It is therefore most pertinent to consider those who are missing out on all four forms of social activity and therefore could be deemed to be at risk of social isolation. We calculated the predicted probabilities of reporting no participation on any of the four dimensions for men in each ethnic group among those without long-term ill health or caring responsibilities and also for those with both long-term ill health and caring responsibilities.[31] Given

---

[29] To explore this point in more detail we ran the regression testing for the effect of ill health and including only basic demographic controls: age, partnership status and the presence or absence of a child under five years of age. Even in such a simple model, ill health was not found to have an association with participation.

[30] We ran a linear regression with an interaction term between ethnicity and ill health in this instance given the difficulty of interpreting coefficients from interactions and determining their statistical significance in logit and probit models (see Ai and Norton, 2005; and for an example of using a linear probability model to get round this problem, see Lindley et al, 2006).

[31] For illustration we compare those without a long-term health condition with those who both have a long-term condition and who are caring. Within the data there were a small number of those in this situation. However, the point of predicted probabilities is heuristic, to show the impact of particular characteristics, given particular sets of characteristics, rather than to match the characteristics to distributions within the data, which are shown in the descriptive statistics. Here the combination of long-term health condition with caring shows the most extreme situation relative to having no such condition and to not being a carer. The combination of ill health and caring also provided consistency in the illustrations across the sexes, since the effect of caring was statistically significant for the sample of men and the effect of ill health was statistically significant for the sample of women.

that Black African men were the only group that stood out as having risks of non-participation that were statistically significantly higher than the White British baseline, we simply compare these two groups. Figure 9 shows that the risk of no participation was significantly higher among Black African men than White British men among those without long-term ill health or caring responsibilities. And, although the confidence intervals are wide for the groups that had ill health or caring responsibilities, Black Africans may again be more likely to lack social participation.

Among women, the story from the quantitative data was slightly different. The effects of qualifications, age and partnership were similar to those for men. Having a child under the age of five was also associated with higher risks of non-participation, but for women the effect was not statistically significant at conventional levels. By contrast with men, however, caring did not appear to reduce participation, but ill health showed a relatively strong – and significant – inhibiting effect.[32] This would seem to fit with the stories that our women respondents were telling us in terms of restrictions on activities. In relation to caring, it may be that as caring is a less exceptional activity for women than for men, it has less of an impact on social activities, especially in the light of the pressures felt by women to maintain household roles, discussed in Chapter 2. Furthermore, it may be that it is differences in the *quality* rather than the quantity of the social contact that are relevant. As with the men, there was no evidence that the *impact* of ill health and caring on social participation varied by ethnic group.

However, there were more striking differences between ethnic groups in levels of non-participation among the women. All three minority ethnic groups had higher risks of non-participation compared with White British women – a pattern that was also suggested in the qualitative work. Again, we illustrate this with predicted probabilities of lacking all four forms of participation by ethnic group and, within group, whether long-term ill and caring (Figure 10).

Figure 9: Predicted probabilities of lack of participation on four measures, White British and Black African men compared

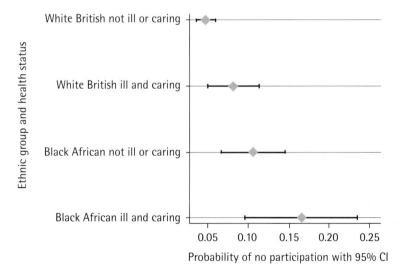

Probability of no participation with 95% CI

Notes: Weighted data; unweighted count for full regression model = 5,321; characteristics are set to: highest qualification is level 3, partnered, no children, in employment, aged 18-40. 'Ill' is used as shorthand for having a long-term health condition and caring is for having caring responsibilities.
Source: 2001 HOCS

[32] However, tests across the two models did not reject the possibility that the coefficients for ill health and caring were in fact the same.

Figure 10: Predicted probabilities of lack of participation on four measures, women from four ethnic groups compared

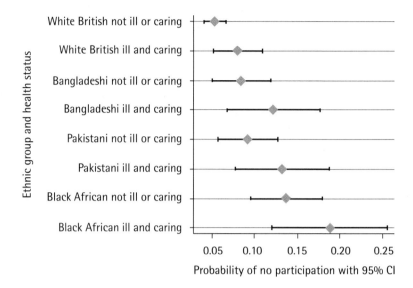

Notes: Weighted data; unweighted count for full regression model = 6,192; characteristics are set to: highest qualification is level 3, partnered, no children, in employment, aged 18-40. 'Ill' is used as shorthand for having a long-term health condition and 'caring' is for having caring responsibilities.
Source: 2001 HOCS

Figure 10 shows a clear ranking of the risks across the groups and their health/caring status; however, the confidence intervals are wide and largely overlap. As with the qualitative data, we can identify patterns but few clear-cut distinctions. The exception is again the Black African women who, with or without long-term ill health, had significantly higher risks of non-participation than their White British counterparts. This again fits with the narratives of our Ghanaian women, several of whom were single mothers working long hours and had little time or opportunity for social participation.

The relevance of income for men's and women's social participation

Our qualitative data highlighted the central role of finances on reduced social participation among those with long-term health conditions and other family members. Organisational membership fees, costs of eating or drinking out or of providing food for visitors, all competed with the costs of maintaining the household, usually on a reduced income.

Quantitative analyses also showed that income is relevant in influencing opportunities for social participation.[33] However, in general, differences in income level did not appear to explain the relationships between the other variables and social participation among men. The exception was Black African men: part of their increased risk of non-participation did seem to be due to financial constraints (since controlling for income in the statistical models decreased the coefficient, although it remained substantial and highly significant).

For women carers, non-participation did not appear to be driven by income (since the coefficient for caring increased once income was included and approached statistical significance). On the other hand, the financial constraints associated with ill health did

---

[33] Due to relatively high levels of non-response, including income in the models reduced sample sizes and thus the chance of finding statistically significant results. Nevertheless, it was instructive to investigate whether coefficients on other variables changed in magnitude once income was included, even if they were not statistically significant. However, note that our models do control for employment status.

appear to be important for women (since the coefficient for ill health halved in size and became statistically insignificant once income level was controlled for). This finding accords with the reports from our female respondents in the qualitative work. Assuming the 'therapeutic' value of social activity is accepted, these findings indicate the need to focus on financial welfare as a route to improved health status for women via greater social contact.

In relation to ethnicity, the higher risks of non-participation among Pakistani women relative to White British women that were identified above were found to be largely explained by differences in income (since the coefficient almost halved when income was controlled for). In contrast, income played some role, but a much smaller one, in explaining the relatively higher risks of non-participation for Bangladeshi and Black African women.

The quantitative analyses therefore suggested that the opportunities for social participation open to Black African men and women, and to a lesser extent Bangladeshi women, were particularly constrained, while those for Pakistani women were heavily determined by income, with those on lower incomes losing out relative to better-off Pakistani women and to White British women on similar incomes.

However, the nature and quality of social contacts, and the ways that these might vary not only with ethnicity but with long-term ill health, cannot be addressed with our quantitative data and are issues we return to below in the section 'The nature, use and effectiveness of social support'.

First, however, we sum up the extent to which men and women in different groups lack all four forms of social participation, and how this varies with ill health, while controlling for income band. In Figure 11 we bring together probabilities from the models for both men

Figure 11: Predicted probabilities of lack of participation on four measures by ethnic group, sex and health status

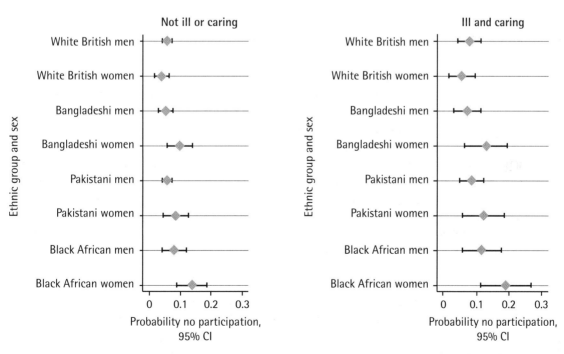

Notes: Weighted data; unweighted counts for full regression model = 3,909 (men), 4,376 (women); characteristics are set to: highest qualification is level 3, partnered, no children, in employment, aged 18-40. 'Ill' stands for those with long-term health conditions and 'caring' for those with caring responsibilities.
Source: 2001 HOCS

and women, and separate the results by health and caring status, to clarify the extent to which men's and women's tendencies to lack social participation are distinct.

From Figure 11, we can see that for the three minority ethnic groups, women's probabilities of lacking all four forms of social participation were higher than men's, but the reverse was the case for White British women and men. In all groups, those with long-term ill health and caring responsibilities had a higher probability of lacking participation than for those without (however, the confidence intervals are relatively wide in many cases). Even so, Black African women stand out as having particularly high risks of non-participation. This finding, although based on the broader category of 'Black African', resonates with the narratives of many of our female Ghanaian respondents.

> *Interviewer:* 'What kind of support would you like to have from your friends?'

> *Respondent:* 'Oh, even eh socially somebody talking to you, if you have somebody to talk to you – somebody to go out with – somebody to do something for you in the house – it's nice but you don't usually get that kind of help.' (Ghanaian woman with long-term condition, 45-49 years)

The nature, use and effectiveness of social support

On the face of it individuals and households may appear to be participating in formal and informal social networks and may not therefore seem isolated or lacking in support. However, the importance of social networks lies in their ability to meet individual members' needs. As Barrera (1982) and others have highlighted, social support must be understood as multidimensional, and the elements that are most significant to an individual commonly change with the onset of long-term ill health. We found that the content of exchanges within networks is commonly restricted, making it difficult for individuals to make claims beyond what is normally expected for any particular network. The experience of long-term ill health changes people's perceptions of social networks as their need for support of various kinds increases and their ability to participate is compromised in a number of related ways.

Respondents' stories suggested three main factors that compromised seeking and receiving effective support: a reluctance to reveal ill health/incapacity and consequent unwillingness to ask for help; demands and expectations of reciprocity; and lack of trust and confidence in the sources of support. While some individuals found ways to access support, for many these concerns effectively limited the extent and benefits of social contact. Both practical and emotional forms of support[34] were identified as important, although clearly this distinction is often an artificial one, particularly perhaps, in relation to a 'good friend'.

Practical support (informational, material, physical assistance)

Although examples of receiving practical help from friends and neighbours with shopping, cooking, cleaning and childcare were found, far more respondents described struggling to complete practical tasks alone, and avoiding seeking practical help from people outside the home.

---

[34] Barrera's (1982) Inventory of Socially Supportive Behaviours identifies four main domains of support: informational (advice, information, feedback) and instrumental (material, physical assistance) – which we have combined into 'practical'; and socialising (taking the mind off things, leisure) and emotional (discussing feelings, expressing concern) – which we have grouped together as 'emotional'. A further dimension relates to support that boosts self-esteem and feelings of being valued, which can again be grouped with the emotional types of support.

'I have never asked for any help from anyone … even in 1997 [when I was very sick] I never asked anyone to help me with my cleaning or cooking. I have always asked for their blessings.' (Bangladeshi woman with long-term condition, 35-39 years)

This reluctance to request support was commonly related to personal pride and a desire to conceal incapacity, rather than a belief that help would not be forthcoming. However, gaining sustained practical support was felt unlikely by several respondents due to people's sympathy waning over time. As one respondent put it: 'I had lots of friends. But I do not have friends anymore. When you are well you have friends but when you are not well … no friends' (Bangladeshi man with long-term condition, 40-44 years).

Clearly, the limits to what people can claim are also tied up with feelings of obligation, reciprocity and rights, factors that vary with the network in question. Earlier work has highlighted the way in which reciprocity among family and wider relatives is an ongoing process and more long term in nature than exchanges between neighbours or groups. Furthermore, family forms that emphasise collectivism mean that exchanges may be given and reclaimed by different family members. These understandings were evident among some of our Bangladeshi and Pakistani respondents. However, obligations did not go unchallenged and reciprocity was not always honoured, even within families. One respondent who had looked after her father-in-law for many years said:

'Like for example in [my daughter's] wedding I needed help. My sister-in-law did not help me a bit. It was her duty to help me. I did so much for her father, and she knows about my illness, and even then she was so indecent not to help me.' (Pakistani woman with long-term condition, 45-49 years)

Expectations of returns (and disappointment) were not specific to these communities, however. One White English woman complained that:

'Helping people out like putting people up 'cause they have nowhere to go, they promised to help out with the electric and things, but then after a few weeks they say, 'I haven't got any money'. They have robbed off us.' (White English woman with long-term condition, 40-44 years)

Several respondents felt that although they had friends and relatives who were there for them, they were not able to provide the required support because of their own commitments to work and family. Also, individuals with long-term conditions tended to need more frequent and a greater degree of support, distinguishing their situation from 'normal' people who might need help only occasionally. Interestingly, a number of respondents across all the communities described not wanting to ask for support because of the need to save their dues for times of more serious need. Despite a general reticence towards seeking support, there was some evidence that women's networks were more productive than men's. For instance, there were examples of households accessing financial support through the networks of women from all four communities.

Several Bangladeshi and Pakistani households had started to withdraw themselves from their earlier networks because they felt unable to cope with the pressures to entertain guests. Similarly, respondents from the White English and Ghanaian communities talked of withdrawing from activities where they could no longer sustain 'expected' behaviours, such as consuming alcohol (prevented by dietary restrictions), buying a round of drinks in the pub (prevented by low income) or dressing up smartly to go out (prevented by low income and/or fatigue).

'If people arrange to meet at a pub you know that you're going to have to go in there and you won't be able to buy a round, if you're lucky you might get yourself one drink so you tend to avoid them. 'We're going to meet at the pub'... 'I'm busy that day, I can't do it'. If they said, like, meet at the park, I would have said yeah.' (White English man with long-term condition, 40-44 years)

Taking favours and not being able to return them made several respondents from across the four communities feel reluctant to ask for support. Seeking financial support from outside the immediate family was considered a particular taboo by many respondents across all groups. Far more respondents reported using credit cards, buying from catalogues or borrowing from the 'tallyman' to spread costs and cover shortfalls. Where money was borrowed from friends there were strict limits to the amount involved: 'Um ... friends, fiver here, fiver there. Nobody's got any money ... it doesn't come through or someone you've borrowed from needs it back' (White English man with long-term condition, 40-44 years).

However, some people succeeded in maintaining reciprocal arrangements through adjusting patterns of entertaining and socialising. One Bangladeshi respondent said that because of his wife's ill health they are unable to cook for friends at home and so they order ready-cooked, take-away food. This clearly has cost implications, however, and so many families may be constrained in relation to such solutions. Others found new ways of reciprocating that were more compatible with their current circumstances, such as providing childcare, and so maintained networks.

'Formal' group membership was often no better at delivering the type of support required by those with health conditions and their families than 'informal' networks. For instance, despite extensive Ghanaian networks and organised groups and a pervasive Christian value of helping individuals in need, the stories of those with long-term conditions suggested that group and organisation affiliations did not often provide extensive support in times of need. For example, members of several Ghanaian religious groups reported receiving spiritual support but that other types of needed help, including practical assistance and financial support, were not forthcoming. Although groups and organisations may require less reciprocation than friendship or kinship-based networks, this sometimes means merely short-term or one-off support. Respondents noted that 'sympathy wears off' and the sense of obligation that permeates the close informal networks of friends and relatives is often not present.

The assumption that participation in groups helps individuals to adapt and access support was challenged by the limited remits of many of the groups that respondents participated in. One such example was a Pakistani women's group, which was explicitly set up to provide a distraction and a place to 'freshen up', rather than a forum in which to share problems. However, this was not true across the board, and we did find examples of groups evolving to meet the needs of its members. For instance, a Pakistani men's group had developed into a forum for benefits advice exchange despite its initial purely social focus.

Gaining access to information and advice on how to live with the health condition in question was a particular issue for many respondents. Few of our respondents were engaged in groups specifically catering for the needs of those with long-term health conditions, and self-management was not a salient aspect of community-level awareness in any of the four communities. This is perhaps surprising, particularly for the Bangladeshis in Tower Hamlets and the Pakistanis in Newham, where there are now widespread 'self-management' or 'expert patient' groups and classes on offer run by both voluntary agencies and the NHS. Furthermore, many respondents expressed particularly ambivalent attitudes towards socialising with individuals having similar conditions. While such networks and groups could potentially provide much-needed advice, downsides were identified including the potential for the individual's state of ill health to become more 'fixed' through dwelling on the subject. In addition, several respondents wanted to access more support, but viewed such groups as offering a space in which to chat and share experiences rather than the practical support that they felt they needed (such as help with benefit applications or housing issues). Few respondents reported that their ill health had led them to establish new social networks; and formal group membership based on ill health identity was particularly unattractive for many. Respondents with mental health conditions even described such organised groups as scary. Among the minority ethnic individuals who were attending ill-health-related groups, most of whom were Bangladeshi or Pakistani, the desire to join seemed to be related as much to a shared ethnic identity as to sharing a common health condition.

But some individuals and families had established networks on the basis of their health condition, and in a small number of cases group membership did seem to be associated with positive adaptation to their changed circumstances. For instance, one White English respondent attended regular craft classes for those with mental ill health and was also active in a local disability group. A Ghanaian woman and her daughter had found a local disease-specific organisation helpful. Moreover, some individuals chose to be pragmatic in their use of formal support: one respondent who was a regular member of a women's group said she did not trust anyone in the group but she found it helpful in providing information on various issues, and that was why she attended. Where respondents were positive about their group/organisational experiences they seemed largely to relate to practical assistance, rather than emotional support.

Emotional support and friendship

An important consideration for respondents across all the ethnic groups was having (or lacking) a 'good friend': someone trustworthy, non-judgemental and empathic. Although most respondents identified people they considered 'friends', far fewer had someone they could rely on for this type of emotional support. In common with earlier work on masculinities (Sixsmith and Boneham, 2002), White English men seemed particularly lacking in confiding, emotionally supportive friendships. As one respondent puts it: 'If I ask someone about their illness [in the pub], they will punch me on my nose. People play poker, not ask about health' (White English man with long-term condition, 45-49 years). Similarly, Bangladeshi and Pakistani men commonly viewed talking about problems as showing weakness, although there were some who had such confiding relationships, and there was a sense that many more would have valued such support.

> '[Y]ou just say friends, you know, everybody busy, you know, if they don't come you don't force anybody. [Sighs] But then she [wife] has her own social circles, she do so much, no problems from her [wife] side, you know … my side, you know, before my own friends, you know, the[re] was R's own friends. Her friends [are] so nice, you know.… Well, you know, I talk [openly] to my missus [wife], that's the only one I suppose.' (Pakistani man, family member, 55-60 years)

In contrast, our Bangladeshi and Pakistani female respondents were more likely to have same-sex friends who were a source of emotional support. For these women, many of their 'friends' were also relatives and a lot of their contact was by telephone rather than in person. The sharing of pain and problems with others was found to be expected in these close female friendships and could be seen as a kind of test of closeness, although disappointment was frequently mentioned, as discussed below. Women in the White English, Pakistani and Bangladeshi communities thus appeared to play an important role in forming and maintaining the type of social networks that provide emotional support in times of need. However, among our Ghanaian female respondents there was a much stronger sense of isolation, and many lacked close supportive relationships.

A small number of respondents cited their friends as a major factor that had helped them come to terms with their ill health. Although these individuals appeared to have had a strong network of friends prior to onset of the condition, there was also evidence that they had actively adjusted their behaviours to find new ways of maintaining social contact and the degree of intimacy in their relationships, through, for example, speaking on the telephone rather than visiting (reflecting the importance of practical coping strategies, as discussed in Chapter 3).

> *Respondent:* 'No, the support has remained constant throughout, that's one good thing … I haven't lost touch with anybody … I would say in one or two friendships it's probably got better….'
>
> *Interviewer:* 'What things would you say have really helped you?'
>
> *Respondent:* 'I think it was knowing, knowing that I had good support from friends and family…. You know, constant phone calls, texts, text messages, the cards, the letters, they were sort of giving me hope, you know, don't give up.' (White English woman with long-term condition, 40-44 years)

Unfortunately, for many others, feelings of mistrust appeared to undermine the usefulness of social networks to individuals and families with long-term ill health. A general lack of trust was noticeable among Ghanaian respondents in their stories. These respondents commonly linked the issue of trust to their vulnerable positions in the UK, as outlined in Chapter 2. Several Bangladeshi and Pakistani respondents also shared stories where their trust was betrayed by a close friend or relative. Prior negative experiences seemed to cause some respondents to be guarded in forming trusted relationships and revealing information, reflecting their feelings of vulnerability (Chapter 3).

> 'Yeah I like to stay private. I don't want everybody to know everything and it's hard to trust people. Sooner or later people just chuck it back in your face, the sad reality of it is that's what they do.' (Pakistani woman, family member, 20-24 years)
>
> "I think it's because of the illness I keep to myself …you can't trust people, few people you can trust, they let you down all the time…. My social life … can't say I have friends.' (Ghanaian woman with long-term condition, 50-54 years)

A mismatch between the support that individuals want and that which they actually receive was commonly reported by respondents, and was also evident when we compared reports of family members with those with ill health themselves. However, it was also evident that several respondents had high expectations from friends and although their stories gave plenty of examples of assistance, they did not feel adequately supported. Several respondents felt that good support was that which was provided without the need to ask. On the other hand, some respondents felt 'smothered' by the support that they received. As noted in Chapter 3, achieving coherence between needs as perceived by 'outsiders' and felt wants is often difficult, as the following quotations illustrate: 'I was crying for help, not asking, they didn't want to help' (Ghanaian woman with long-term condition, 45-49 years); 'She [girlfriend] was trying to be helpful but the more helpful she got … the more helpless I felt….' (White English man with long-term condition, 40-44 years).

Conclusions

Maintaining social participation and receiving adequate and appropriate social support were major concerns for many of our respondents in the qualitative work. Many felt that ill health had serious consequences for their social lives, and many felt poorly supported. Although neither the qualitative nor the quantitative data suggested important differences in the *extent* to which ill health affects social participation across the ethnic groups, the dimensions of social life that concerned individuals did vary by ethnicity.

Over and above social contact, the *content* of exchanges within social networks is crucial if they are to be perceived as supportive by those living with ill health. Although it is clear that individuals value emotional support, nevertheless it was noticeable that when referring to lack of support most respondents tended to focus on practical and material aspects, reflecting the fact that long-term ill health is often interlinked with other problems and that financial insecurity is a central worry for many.

Health status matters across ethnic groups for women and caring status for men; but the effects of health and caring do not appear to vary with the ethnic group of the person affected. The message would appear to be that if we are concerned about lack of participation in its own right and its impact in shaping long-term health outcomes, focusing on income maintenance will improve the situation of women with long-term health conditions and Pakistani women in particular; but that the lower levels of participation among Black African men and women might require more targeted interventions to improve their welfare in this respect.

Informal networks were generally not good at providing the kind of longstanding support that was needed. In the fieldwork areas, many respondents were surrounded by relatives and neighbours facing similar financial insecurity and felt unable to claim assistance from those who 'had their own lives and problems'. The mismatch between expectations and actuality was also a common theme; for instance a social occasion could turn out to be stressful through the physical and/or financial demands it created.

Formal groups and organisations did not appear better at meeting the needs of those with long-term ill health and their families. This is both because groups fail to provide the range of support that is needed, and because some individuals do not find group membership attractive. There was some evidence that language barriers and perceptions of cultural difference may act to exclude individuals from particular groups (for instance many of the disease-specific groups run by voluntary organisations are White-dominated, and there was evidence that even among 'Asian' groups there may be inclusion/exclusion along the lines of religion, even if this is not overt). However, reluctance on the part of individuals to identify as 'ill' and to join groups that are defined by ill health state appeared to be a more significant factor that limits participation, and consequent access to information and valued support.

These findings suggest the need for varied types and modes of support provision, and a need for groups/organisations to take a holistic approach, recognising the interconnections between different aspects of people's lives. Internet support and telephone helplines were mentioned by some respondents, but do not seem to be widely accessed. Home visitors and neighbourhood drop-in centres were not mentioned, but might be attractive options for those more constrained in their movements. Women in our minority ethnic groups appeared to face particular difficulties with respect to securing adequate support. The relative isolation of Ghanaian women in terms of range, intensity and quality of social contact was pronounced. Bangladeshi and Pakistani women appeared to be less isolated, but did not necessarily find their social contact to be supportive. Working with existing groups to expand their remit may be useful. However, more innovative ways of reaching those in greatest need are clearly required.

7

Relevance of findings for national policy

Introduction

The findings presented in this report have relevance for a number of strands of current UK health and social policy, including:

- the welfare-to-work agenda, and specifically the planned interventions to increase the number of 'sick or disabled' people who are in work set out in the 2006 Welfare Reform Green Paper (DWP, 2006a);
- the DWP's Public Service Agreement target on minority ethnic groups' employment, and the related work of the (cross-departmental) Ethnic Minority Employment Task Force;
- the carers' agenda, specifically the 2004 Carers (Equal Opportunities) Act;
- the disability rights agenda and the 1995 and 2005 Disability Discrimination Acts; and
- the health agendas around patient choice and responsibility and reducing the burden of long-term care, specifically the Public Health White Paper *Choosing health: Making healthy choices easier* (DH, 2004a) and the White Paper *Our health, our care, our say: A new direction for community services* (DH, 2006).

Current government policy considers work to be the central route by which individuals and households move out of poverty. This assumption underpins much other policy relating to the welfare of working age-people and therefore forms a central part of our discussion here.

Benefit entitlement and take-up

Increasing awareness and access to (accurate) information

A majority of individuals were heavily reliant on informal social ties for access to benefit information and therefore the extent and accuracy of information varied with personal networks. There was also clearly much misinformation circulating, which needs to be combated. Networks based around health status itself tended not to be regarded as either inherently meaningful or as providing effective sources of advice and support. Approaches that support and expand the remit of community networks developed on the basis of common ethnicity may be effective routes to dissemination of information and advice for some groups.[35] However, our work highlighted variation between 'groups' in the extent to which ethnic-specific infrastructure exists that could be built upon, as well as in the ease with which issues of ill health and finances can be discussed openly. There is a need for multiple avenues of publicity to be used to ensure wide access to information. Community radio stations are popular among many minority ethnic individuals and may be a useful

---

[35] The desirability of such ethnic-specific approaches is discussed below.

medium. Religious centres (mosques and churches) might also be used. In addition, however, 'mainstream' state agencies and providers across the health and social welfare arenas need to do a better job at publicising available ill-health-related benefits (including DLA) and ensuring awareness across all communities.

Overcoming aversions to claiming

Claims for appropriate benefits are also impeded by concerns about the desirability and legitimacy of claiming sickness benefits. Benefits can clearly play an important role in validation of ill health. Thus, having claims disallowed can also cause difficulties in the positive adaptation to living with ill health or justifying it to self/others. Furthermore, the negative associations of 'malingering' that have been associated with sickness benefits can make the experience of claiming and receiving benefit uncomfortable. Clearly, not all individuals with long-term health conditions are eligible for benefit support, and some who are eligible actively choose not to claim such benefits. However, wider community and societal pressures that construct such claims as illegitimate and undesirable clearly act as obstacles to claiming for many whose standard of living might be helped by benefit income. Increased attention is needed to the ways in which government policy directives (and resultant practices at local level) might encourage, rather than deter, eligible claimants.

Increasing access to specialist support

Obtaining benefits was a struggle for many respondents, even when they felt they had a strong case for entitlement. Access to independent advice and specialist support was rare and clearly needs to be more widely available across all groups, if take-up of benefit is to be improved.

Improving the appropriateness of health status assessments

Some respondents felt that GPs were reluctant to certify them as 'sick' or 'unfit for work', even when they perceived their own heath condition as clearly precluding employment. The intention that GPs should further stress the benefits of work and discourage sickness absence/inactivity may risk putting the patient–doctor relationship under strain, and should be implemented with caution.

The Welfare Reform Green Paper (DWP, 2006a) still fails to recognise employability as a contingent and dynamic process, dependent not only on the condition, which can itself change over time, but also on the other characteristics/skills of the potential employee and the labour market options available, which are also liable to change. The continuing use of capacity for (any) work as a yardstick for assessing benefit entitlement is overly narrow, potentially stigmatising and unfair to those who, much as they would like work, fail to get it (and there is plenty of evidence on quite how hard it is for those with a long-term condition/disability to obtain work).

The levels of pain and fatigue associated with long-term health conditions were vividly illustrated by our respondents, as well as the fact that symptoms could be intermittent. A further important issue was the frequency of medical appointments and intensity of contact with health services, making availability for work difficult and often unpredictable. Assessments do not necessarily take full account of these issues when judging capacity and suitability for work. Assessments may need to be more flexible in the way they approach long-term health conditions and evaluate their impact on 'fitness for work'. A greater stress on understanding and getting better information on intermittent symptoms and fatigue and the way that they might interfere with the performance of a job, or be exacerbated by employment, would be valuable.

Redressing the balance in current policy focus

Much of the above discussion indicates the need for the reform agenda to be accompanied by an equal stress on entitlement and supporting people in fully claiming benefits for which they are eligible and which will at least partially ease some of the stresses associated with chronic ill health. How to support take-up by those with apparent entitlement is currently not subject to attention. The absence of discussion of DLA in recent policy documents is also a worrying omission since this benefit was found to make a significant improvement to the lives of a number of respondents and apparent take-up rates remain extremely low. Furthermore, the concern that receipt of IB/IS in and of itself leads to marginalisation and exclusion from employment opportunities seems unwarranted. Receipt of sickness-related benefits was not necessarily in conflict with a working identity, with several respondents viewing receipt of IB as an appropriate, but ideally temporary, measure. In fact, in some cases, being labelled as 'fit for work' and therefore receiving Jobseeker's Allowance, rather than IB/IS, was a factor that exacerbated their feelings of marginalisation and frustration precisely because their health condition and specialist needs were not acknowledged by the system. Likewise, the suggestion that increased levels of IB/IS entitlement over time is a 'perverse' incentive to remain out of work does not reflect the experiences of our respondents. Instead, such increased payments are entirely warranted given the ways in which prolonged low income is associated with a gradual deterioration in living standards as household appliances, clothes and so on wear out and break down.

The appropriateness of work for those with long-term health conditions

Tailoring support for job search and training

Employment remains a core part of identity to many with long-term ill health and many identify work as bringing varied advantages over and above income. However, these perceptions vary with stage of life and with the type of work that can be carried out or is anticipated. Job-search support and help with the transition to employment may be critical for some, but for others it may seem irrelevant. Appropriate targeting of support and considering the full range of options, without falling back on stereotyping assumptions, is important. In addition, people with chronic health conditions need to be seen in the context of their families and households – the support that they are receiving at home, and the ways that their employment may impact on the well-being or employment of those around them, for example if they need help getting to the work place or preparing for work. An approach to job search and job training that links holistically to social support provision and carers' assessments is recommended.

Increased attention to quality of employment and job retention

Contrary to the assertion that work brings with it many benefits other than higher income, 'poor' jobs can in fact exacerbate health conditions and the stress relating to combining work with long-term ill health in the first place. Identifying appropriate employment, rather than any employment, is important for the well-being of those with a long-term health condition and is likely to aid retention. It is staying in work, as well as getting into work, that is important, and indications are that health conditions make staying in work harder and that this also varies by ethnicity. A stronger focus on retention is likely to be effective for minority ethnic employment targets as well.

Increased recognition of obstacles to employment and alternative positive 'outcomes'

While our evidence did not indicate that the impact of health conditions is greater for those from certain ethnic groups, nevertheless combinations of obstacles to employment resulting from ill health, the ethnic penalty and other characteristics, such as skills levels, can result in very low chances of employment for some. It is important to recognise the reality of these limited opportunities (and how they can impact on motivations) without being fatalistic. What is an 'appropriate' response to long-term ill health in relation to aims for labour market participation may vary with the extent of the obstacles to participation. Regarding ill health and consequent economic inactivity as a stage of life may represent positive adaptation for some individuals. This needs to be recognised when arguing for the value of work in relation to self-esteem and overall welfare. There may be trade-offs at the individual level between ongoing low income and the stresses of repeated rejection. In addition, uncertainty or cycling between employment and non-employment can bring its own costs.

Voluntary work may offer an important 'alternative' to paid work and may provide relatively unstressful validation of self, but it cannot necessarily be seen as a 'stepping stone' to employment. While it may prove to be so in some cases, in others it can be (felt as) an end in itself. Supporting those with long-term health conditions to engage in such work without loss (or fear of loss) of crucial benefits, is therefore important. The therapeutic benefits as well as the gain to the community of such activity should be actively recognised.

As we noted above, the welfare reform agenda needs to address the question of potential inability of those deemed 'capable' of work to actually find a job (or a stable job), and consider what levels of support might be appropriate in such circumstances – rather than assuming the current overwhelmingly punitive stance.

Realistic assessment of and support to employers' roles

Our research confirmed the point that employers have an important role in supporting individuals to remain in work or in offering flexible opportunities. The Welfare Reform Green Paper (DWP, 2006a) emphasised the need to focus on people before they became economically inactive by engaging employers and instituting appropriate workplace practices. This is a welcome emphasis. However, some jobs will simply be inappropriate for those with a long-term health condition or particular health conditions. And small employers may have more difficulty in adjusting. Consideration needs to be given to the nature of available opportunities, how to support transitions to different types of work and related training opportunities, as well as to encouraging and supporting employers to offer flexibility in hours, tasks and so on. There are also difficult issues around confidentiality and privacy and fear of labelling that may make employees reluctant to seek or take up tailored provision. And some of our respondents raised concerns that requiring too much flexibility from employers could result in their reluctance to employ sick and disabled people at all. There is clearly a tension between employers' needs for a reliable workforce and the unpredictable and disruptive (to their own lives as well as their employment) nature of much long-term ill health.

Our research did not take place in a Pathways to Work area. Given the positive results coming out of the Pathways initiative, it is important to consider how that experience may be relevant to the issues considered here, and how they are followed up.

The appropriateness of work for those caring for someone with a long-term health condition

Supporting family members and carers into employment

Caring may substantially limit the amount and types of work that individuals are able to undertake. In addition, the demands of caring are not necessarily predictable, with some of those with long-term conditions needing family members to accompany them to hospital appointments and so on. Additionally, part-time work, which is often the only option, typically offers low rewards. Supporting carers to train/retrain may increase their options; and the flexibility of employers is also crucial to carers as well as to those with a chronic health condition themselves. A more proactive approach to the use of carers' assessments to facilitate flexible forms of participation would be welcomed.

Recognising competing priorities for household welfare

On the other hand, working may simply be regarded as inappropriate. The demands of caring may cause individuals to give up work. For those who are already not in work through, for example, family responsibilities, the substitution of roles (for example swapping family care for employment) is not always viable or perceived as such. Perceptions of care/support needed and desirability of family role substitution were found to vary between households (and there were some ethnic differentials here). However, what is most pertinent is the extent to which households combine both dependent children and adults with a chronic health condition. The issues facing such households cross ethnic boundaries, even if the distribution of such households varies dramatically across ethnic groups. This highlights the fact that ill health has to be regarded as affecting whole families rather than 'simply' the individual. Work may not be regarded by those who are carrying out multiple caring roles as the most appropriate way of maintaining or enhancing the welfare of the family and of its different members. Employment policies need to be sensitive to the differences in configurations of households and, when engaging with aims for abolishing child poverty, they need to adequately consider how the overall welfare of children, including older children, is best maintained.

Managing long-term ill health

Providing diverse modes of support

Despite government emphasis on providing patients with better information (DH, 2004b) our data suggested that understanding and accessing appropriate information concerning their condition, its implications and its management are still a major problem for many people with long-term health conditions (and their carers). In addition, reluctance to 'dwell' on ill health may reduce individuals' efficacy in accessing appropriate information. The need for both mental adjustment to having a long-term condition and the development of practical strategies (for day-to-day living and forward planning) was highlighted for positive adaptation to the health condition to be achieved. Furthermore, for many respondents, concerns about financial insecurity and hardship, immigration issues, or family disputes, overshadowed ill-health-related symptoms, and support services must therefore recognise the complex realities of people's daily lives and offer support in a holistic fashion. Few of our respondents were receiving any kind of 'formal' support to positively adapt to living with a long-term condition and many felt isolated, unsupported and lacking control over their lives. Again, using existing networks based around shared ethnicity, rather than around specific illnesses or the experience of being ill, may provide a fruitful route for the effective dissemination of information and support. However, it is clear that group-based provision will not suit everyone and there is a need for diverse modes of support to those living with long-term health conditions. There were also concerns that community care provision was not adept at taking account of individual circumstances. The importance of tailoring provision through case management needs to be recognised. At the same time the stress in the Department of Health literature on individual responsibility (DH, 2004a) needs to be tempered by a recognition of the way society contributes to the construction of ill health and (in)capacity.

Giving particular attention to mental ill health

Throughout the report we highlighted the particular difficulties faced by those with mental health conditions, although the physical/mental distinction was not clear cut, with mental illness, particularly depression, often accompanying physical ill health. Mental ill health can be harder to legitimise to oneself and others, and the high levels of stigma associated with mental illness can contribute to lack of acknowledgement of the condition by the individual and their family. This may lead to isolation even within apparently well-resourced communities. It can also be more difficult to demonstrate benefit eligibility with a mental health condition, while the difficulties of claiming can be exacerbated by the health condition or increase anxiety. At the same time, rates of employment among those with mental health conditions are exceptionally low. While policy recognises high levels of mental illness, it is important that this recognition is accompanied by an understanding of the way wider society (including other domains of policy itself) contributes to the exclusion of those with mental illness and prescriptions for how this might be overcome. The healthy workplace agenda may help those with mental health conditions to remain in work, although tensions between revealing and concealing illness will be heightened with mental illness. For those not working, there is an important role for validating both the reality of their problems, through adequate financial support and through recognising alternative roles and contributions. It is also important to engage with communities where the 'culture of silence' is particularly strong to help avoid the isolation that can exacerbate their and their carers' difficulties.

Tackling minority ethnic disadvantage

Recognising similarities and differences across and within ethnic 'groups'

The findings presented in the preceding chapters have drawn attention to the complex relationships that exist between long-term ill health, poverty and ethnicity. It was not true to say that minority ethnic status uniformly exacerbated the relationships between ill health and dimensions of poverty. Importantly, in Chapter 4, we highlighted the fact that the *effect* of ill health on employment did not differ in magnitude between the ethnic groups. Moreover, there were many commonalities across ethnic groups in the ways in which individuals experienced ill health and the resources they sought to draw on in coping with their health condition. Nevertheless, in terms of key outcomes – that is, levels of employment and receipt of sickness benefits – there was evidence that individuals belonging to the three minority ethnic groups under study are commonly disadvantaged when compared with White individuals with comparable characteristics. In addition, there were important differences between the three minority ethnic groups in several respects, particularly in terms of household composition and household roles; employment types; patterns of socialising and social support; and community-level resources. Our qualitative work suggested that a number of factors converge to place Ghanaians (particularly the more recent migrants) with long-term health conditions at particular risk of isolation and financial hardship. However, despite evidence of some differences between the ethnic groups in 'ways of being and doing' (attitudes, preferences and behaviours) that had a bearing on the experience of ill health, we should not overlook the significant heterogeneity that was also apparent *within* our identified 'groups'. Gendered differences were evident across a range of areas of investigation and often took distinct forms in the different ethnic groups, as did patterns by age. Time since migration, and consequent access to formal and informal support, was another important factor. Quantitative work also illustrated the ways in which relationships between ethnicity and dimensions of poverty were contingent upon income level and education. Such heterogeneity would no doubt have been even more obvious in our qualitative work had we included a more socioeconomically diverse sample. Furthermore, we found evidence that the ethnic 'groups' chosen for analysis were not always meaningful, with inclusion within subgroups at times being more relevant for individuals' access to resources, particularly among the Ghanaians (who were linguistically and socioeconomically diverse) and the Pakistanis. In addition, our findings illustrated the ways in which 'cultural norms' are open to change; as in the case of our Pakistani community where more positive attitudes towards benefit receipt had arisen with clusters of individuals all in receipt of DLA being found. The study's findings therefore caution against assuming uniform patterns of disadvantage across minority ethnic groups. Instead, analysts and policy makers must carefully consider what ethnicity implies in particular contexts and for particular outcomes of interest. Furthermore, as Ahmad argues (1996, p 190), it is important to recognise culture as being 'a flexible resource for living' rather than portraying it as something that 'mechanistically determine[s] people's behaviours and actions', and to consider ethnic differentials within the context of wider social, historical, economic and political factors.

Identifying routes to supporting those in greatest need

Our findings confirmed that, whether we like it or not, UK society does currently make a big deal of ethnic (and increasingly religious) identity. Social networks were dominated by co-ethnic ties and our minority ethnic groups tended to be concentrated in particular residential areas and occupational sectors. This means that even where patterns and predictors appear superficially similar across ethnic groups, outcomes may diverge (as in the case of social networks yielding differential information on benefits, discussed in Chapter 5), and/or avenues to intervention may need to be ethnically differentiated (as in the case of specific language support needed by individuals whose English is poor). As discussed above, seeking support and accessing services on the basis of shared ethnic identity was meaningful for many of the minority ethnic individuals. Furthermore, we found evidence that particular types of intervention may be needed more by some groups, or subgroups, than others. For instance, there was evidence that Ghanaian (and Black African) women with long-term ill health are at particular risk of social isolation and may face particular constraints to combining household work, childcare and paid work. While the above factors might argue in favour of ethnically delineated services and interventions, there is clearly a need to avoid stereotyping, while acknowledging dimensions of support that *may* be of most relevance to particular individuals. In addition, it is important to consider the implications of such an approach for the broader goals of social inclusion and community cohesion. Furthermore, a focus on such 'community-based' solutions may mean that government agencies take their legal obligation to ensure accessible services for all less seriously. It is clearly important to meet the needs of minority ethnic individuals without furthering their marginalisation and isolation from 'mainstream' services and opportunities. Indeed, it may be the case that individuals with long-term ill health would particularly benefit from expanding their links beyond their 'own community', for instance, in relation to finding employment that is more compatible with the needs of a long-term condition or accessing support that does not imply reciprocal obligations.

References

Adamson, J. (2005) 'Combining qualitative and quantitative designs', in A. Bowling and S. Abraham (eds) *Handbook of health research methods: Investigation, measurement and analysis*, Maidenhead: Open University Press.

Adelman, L., Middleton, S. and Ashworth, K. (2003) *Britain's poorest children: Severe and persistent poverty and social exclusion*, London: Save the Children.

Ahmad, W.I.U. (1996) 'The trouble with culture', in D. Kelleher and S. Hillier (eds) *Researching cultural differences in health*, London: Routledge, 190-219.

Ahmad, W.I.U. (2000) 'Introduction', in W.I.U. Ahmad (ed) *Ethnicity, disability and chronic illness*, Buckingham: Open University Press, 1-11.

Ai, C. and Norton, E.C. (2003) 'Interaction terms in logic and probit models', *Economics Letters*, 80(1), 123-9.

Alcock, P., Beatty, C., Fothergill, S., Macmillan, R. and Yeandle, S. (2003) *Work to welfare: How men become detached from the labour market*, Cambridge: Cambridge University Press.

Anderson, J.M., Elfert, H. and Lai, M (1989) 'Ideology in the clinical context: chronic illness, ethnicity and the discourse on normalisation, *Sociology of Health and Illness*, 11, 253-78.

Anderson, R. and Bury, M. (1988) *Living with chronic illness: The experience of patients and their families*, London: Unwin Hyman.

Arrow, J.O. (1996) 'Estimating the influence of health as a risk factor on unemployment: a survival analysis of employment durations for workers surveyed in the German Socio-Economic Panel (1984-1990)', *Social Science and Medicine*, 42(12), 1651-9.

Ashworth, K., Hartfree, Y. and Stephenson, A. (2001) *Well enough to work?*, DWP Research Report No. 145, Leeds: Corporate Document Services/The Stationery Office.

Atkin, K. and Chattoo, S. (2006) 'Approaches to conducting qualitative research in ethnically diverse populations', in J. Nazroo (ed) *Health and social research in multiethnic societies*, London: Routledge, 95-115.

Atkin, K. and Rollings, J. (1996) 'Looking after their own? Family care giving among South Asian and Afro-Caribbean communities', in W. I. U Ahmad and K. Atkin (eds) *'Race' and community care*, Buckingham: Oxford University Press.

Bacon, J. (2002) 'Moving between sickness and unemployment', *Labour Market Trends*, 2002, 195-205.

Bailey, N. (2006) 'Does work pay? Employment, poverty and social exclusion from social relations', in C. Pantazis, D. Gordon and R. Levitas (eds) *Poverty and social exclusion in Britain: The millennium survey*, Bristol: The Policy Press.

Baldwin, S. (1985) *The costs of caring: Families with disabled children*, London: Routledge and Kegan Paul.

Ballard, R. (1996) 'Negotiating race and ethnicity: exploring the implications of the 1991 Census', *Patterns of Prejudice*, 30(3), 3-33.

Barnard, H. and Pettigrew, N. (2003) *Delivering benefits and services for black and minority ethnic older people*, Leeds: Corporate Document Services.

Barrera, M. (1982) 'Social support in the adjustment of pregnant adolescents', in B. Gottlieb (ed) *Social networks and social support*, Thousand Oaks, CA: Sage Publications, 69-96.

Bartley, M. and Lewis, I. (2002) 'Accumulated labour market disadvantage and limiting long-term illness: data from the 1971-1991 Office for National Statistics' Longitudinal Study', *International Journal of Epidemiology*, 31(2), 336-41.

Basu, A. and Altinay, E. (2003) *Family and work in minority ethnic businesses*, Bristol/York: The Policy Press/Joseph Rowntree Foundation.

Beatty, C. and Fothergill, S. (2002) 'Hidden unemployment among men: a case study', *Regional Studies*, 36(8), 811-23.

Beatty, C. and Fothergill, S. (2005) 'The diversion from 'unemployment' to 'sickness' across British regions and districts', *Regional Studies*, 39(7), 837-54.

Beatty, C., Fothergill, S. and MacMillan, R. (2000) 'A theory of employment, unemployment and sickness', *Regional Studies*, 34(1), 617-30.

Berkman, L.F., Melchior, M., Chastang, J.F., Niedhammer, I., Leclerc, A. and Goldberg, M. (2004) 'Social integration and mortality: a prospective study of French employees of Electricity of France-Gas of France: the GAZAL cohort', *American Journal of Epidemiology*, 15(2), 167-74.

Berthoud, R. (2000) 'Ethnic employment penalties in Britain', *Journal of Ethnic and Migration Studies*, 26(3), 389-416.

Berthoud, R. (2003) *Multiple disadvantage in employment: A quantitative analysis*, York: Joseph Rowntree Foundation/York Publishing Services.

Berthoud, R. (2006) *The employment rates of disabled people*, DWP Research Report No. 298, London: HMSO.

Berthoud, R. and Blekesaune, M. (2006) *Persistent employment disadvantage, 1974-2003*, ISER Working Paper 2006-9, Colchester: University of Essex.

Berthoud, R., Lakey, J. and McKay, S. (1993) *The economic problems of disabled people*, London: Policy Studies Institute.

Blackaby, D.H., Drinkwater, S., Leslie, D.G. and Murphy, P.D. (1997) 'A picture of male and female unemployment among Britain's ethnic minorities', *Scottish Journal of Political Economy*, 44(2), 182-97.

Blackaby, D.H., Leslie, D.G., Murphy, P.D. and O'Leary, N.C. (1999) 'Unemployment among Britain's ethnic minorities', *Manchester School*, 67, 1-20.

Blackaby, D.H., Leslie, D.G., Murphy, P.D. and O'Leary, N.C. (2002) 'White/ethnic minority earnings and employment differentials in Britain: evidence from the LFS', *Oxford Economic Papers*, 54, 270-97.

Blackaby, D.H., Leslie, D.G., Murphy, P.D. and O'Leary, N.C. (2005) 'Born in Britain: how are native ethnic minorities faring in the British labour market', *Economics Letters*, 88, 370-5.

Bloch, A. (1993) *Access to benefits: The information needs of minority ethnic groups*, London: PSI.

Bloch, A. (1997) 'Ethnic inequality and social security', in A. Walker and C. Walker (eds) *Britain divided: The growth of social exclusion in the 1980s and 1990s*, London: CPAG, 111-22.

Bound, J., Waidmann, T., Schoenbaum, M. and Bingenheimer, B.J. (2003) 'The labour market consequences of race differences in health', *Milbank Quarterly*, 81(3), 441-73.

Bradby, H. (2003) 'Describing ethnicity in health research', *Ethnicity and Health*, 8, 5-13.

Braddock, D. and Parish, S. (2001) 'An institutional history of disability', in G. Albrecht, K. Seelman and M Bury (eds) *Handbook of disability studies*, Thousand Oaks, CA: Sage Publications, 11-69.

Burchardt, T. (2000a) 'The dynamics of being disabled', *Journal of Social Policy*, 29, 645-68.

Burchardt, T. (2000b) *Enduring economic exclusion: Disabled people, income and work*, York: Joseph Rowntree Foundation.

Bury, M. (1991) 'The sociology of chronic illness: a review of research and prospects', *Sociology of Health and Illness*, 13(4), 451-68.

Bury, M., Newbould, J. and Taylor, D. (2005) *A rapid review of the current state of knowledge regarding lay-led self-management of chronic illness*, London: National Institute for Health and Clinical Excellence.

Campbell, R., Pound, P., Pope, C., Britten, N., Roisin, P., Morgan, M. and Donovan, J. (2003) 'Evaluating meta-ethnography: a synthesis on lay experiences of diabetes and diabetes care', *Social Science and Medicine*, 56, 671-84.

Charmaz, K. (2000) 'Experiencing chronic illness', in G.L. Albrecht, R. Fizpatrick and S.C. Scrimshaw (eds) *Handbook of social studies in health and medicine*, London: Sage Publications, 277-92.

Chattoo, S. and Ahmad, W. (2003) 'The meaning of cancer: illness, biography and social identity', in D. Kelleher and G. Cahill (eds) *Identity and health*, London: Routledge.

Clark, K. and Drinkwater, S. (2005) *Dynamics and diversity: Ethnic employment differences in England and Wales, 1991-2001*, IZA Discussion Paper 1698, Bonn: IZA.

Cooper, H., Arber, S., Fee, L. and Ginn, J. (1999) *The influence of social support and social capital on health: A review and analysis of British data*, London: Health Education Authority.

Courtens, A.M., Stevens, F., Crebolder, H. and Philipsen, H. (1996) 'Longitudinal study on quality of life and social support in cancer patients', *Cancer Nursing*, 9(3), 162-9.

Craig, G. (2004) 'Citizenship, exclusion and older people', *Journal of Social Policy*, 33, 95-114.

Craig, P. (1991) 'Cash and benefits: a review of research on take-up of income related benefits', *Journal of Social Policy*, 10, 537-66.

Davidson, K.P., Pennebaker, J.W. and Dickerson, S.S. (2000) 'Who talks? The social psychology of illness support groups', *American Psychologist*, 55(2), 205-17.

Dench, G., Young, M. and Gavron, K. (2006) *The new East End: Kinship, race and conflict*, London: Profile Books.

DH (Department of Health) (2004a) *Choosing health: Making healthy choices easier*, London: HMSO.

DH (2004b) *Better information, better choices, better health: Putting information at the centre of health*, London: DH.

DH (2005) *Supporting people with long term conditions: An NHS and social care model to support local innovation and integration*, Long-term Conditions Team, Leeds: DH.

DH (2006) *Our health, our care, our say: A new direction for community services*, London: HMSO.

Drewett, A., Olsen, R. and Parker, G. (1994) *Community care and informal carers*, Leicester: Nuffield Community Care Studies Unit, University of Leicester.

DWP (Department for Work and Pensions) (2003a) *Pathways to work: Helping people into employment: The government's response and action plan*, London: HMSO.

DWP (2003b) *Measuring child poverty*, London: HMSO.

DWP (2006a) *A new deal for welfare: Empowering people to work*, London: HMSO.

DWP (2006b) *Income related benefits: Estimates of take-up in 2003/2004*, London: DWP.

Eade, J. (1997) 'Keeping the options open: Bangladeshi in a global city', in A. Kershen (ed) *London: The promised land*, Aldershot: Avebury, 91-105.

Easterlow, D. and Smith, S. (2003) 'Health and employment: towards a New Deal', *Policy & Politics*, 31(4), 511-33.

Eng, P.M., Rimm, E.B., Fitzmaurice, G. and Kawachi, I. (2002) 'Social ties and change in social ties in relation to subsequent total and cause-specific mortality and coronary artery disease incidence in men', *American Journal of Epidemiology*, 155(8), 700-9.

Falkingham, F. (1985) *Take-up of benefits: A literature review*, Nottingham: Benefits Research Unit, University of Nottingham.

Fieldhouse, E. and Hollywood, E. (1999) 'Life after mining: hidden unemployment and changing patterns of economic activity among miners in England and Wales 1981-91', *Work, Employment and Society*, 13, 483-502.

Fry, V. and Stark, G. (1993) *The take-up of means-tested benefits 1984-90*, London: IFS.

Gardner, K. (2002) *Age, narrative and migration: The life course and life histories amongst Bengali elders in London*, Oxford: Berg.

Gordon, D., Adelman, L., Ashworth, K., Bradshaw, J., Levitas, R., Middleton, S., Pantazis, C., Patsios, D., Payne, S., Townsend, P. and Williams, J. (2000) *Poverty and social exclusion in Britain*, York: Joseph Rowntree Foundation.

Gordon, P. and Newnham, A. (1985) *Passport to benefits? Racism in social security*, London: CPAG/Runnymede Trust.

Grant, G., Ramcharan, P. and Flynn, M. (2007: forthcoming) 'Resilience in families with children and adult members with intellectual disabilities: tracing elements of a psycho-social model', *Journal of Allied Research in Intellectual Disabilities*.

Haskey, J. (1997) 'Population review: the ethnic minority and overseas-born populations of Great Britain', *Population Trends*, 88, 13-30.

Hawe, P. and Sheill, A. (2000) 'Social capital and health promotion: a review', *Social Science and Medicine*, 51(6), 871-5.

Heath, A. and Cheung, S.Y. (2006) *Ethnic penalties in the labour market: Employers and discrimination*, DWP Research Report No. 341, Leeds: Corporate Document Services.

Hedges, A. and Sykes, W. (2001) *Moving between sickness and work*, DWP Research Report No. 151, Leeds: Corporate Document Services.

Higginbottom, G.M.A. (2006) ''Pressure of life': ethnicity as a mediating factor in mid-life and older peoples' experience of high blood pressure', *Sociology of Health and Illness*, 28, 1-28.

Holahan, C.J., Moos, R.H., Holahan, C.K. and Brennan, P.L. (1995) 'Social support, coping and depressive symptoms in a late-middle-aged sample of patients reporting cardiac symptoms', *Health Psychology*, 14(2), 152-63.

House of Commons Work and Pensions Committee (2005) *Delivery of services to ethnic minority clients*, 6 April, House of Commons Paper No. 268, London: The Stationery Office.

Hussain, F. and Cochrane, R. (2004) 'Depression in South Asian women living in the UK: a review of the literature with implications for service provision', *Transcultural Psychiatry*, 41(2), 253-70.

Jenkins, R. (1994) 'Rethinking ethnicity: identity, categorization and power', *Ethnic and Racial Studies*, 17(2), 197-223.

Jenkins, S.P. and Rigg, J.A. (2001) *The dynamics of poverty in Britain*, DWP Research Report No. 157, Leeds: Corporate Document Services/The Stationery Office.

Jenkins, S.P. and Rigg, J.A. (2004) 'Disability and disadvantage: selection, onset and duration effects', *Journal of Social Policy*, 33(3), 479-501.

Karlsen, S. (2004) 'Black like Beckham? Moving beyond definitions of ethnicity based on skin colour and ancestry', *Ethnicity and Health*, 9, 107-38.

Karlsen, S. and Nazroo, J. (2006) 'Defining and measuring ethnicity and race', in J. Nazroo (ed) *Health and social research in multiethnic societies*, London: Routledge, 20-38.

Katbamna, S., Bhakta, P. and Parker, G. (2000) 'Perceptions of disability and care-giving relationships in South Asian communities', in W.I.U. Ahmad (ed) *Ethnicity, disability and chronic illness*, Buckingham: Open University Press, 12-27.

Kawachi, I. and Berkman, L.F. (2001) 'Social ties and mental health', *Journal of Urban Health*, 78(3), 458-67.

Law, I., Hylton, C., Karmani, A. and Deacon, A. (1994) *Racial equality and social security service delivery: A study of the perceptions and experiences of black and minority ethnic people eligible for benefit in Leeds*, Leeds: University of Leeds.

Lawton, J. (2003) 'Lay experience of health and illness: past research and future agendas', *Sociology of Health and Illness*, 25, 23-40.

Levitas, R. (2006) 'The concept and measurement of social exclusion', in C. Pantazis, D. Gordon and R. Levitas (eds) *Poverty and social exclusion in Britain: The millennium survey*, Bristol: The Policy Press, 123-60.

Lindley, J., Dale, A. and Dex, S. (2006) 'Ethnic differences in women's employment: the changing role of qualifications', *Oxford Economic Papers*, 58, 351-78.

Locker, D. (1983) *Disability and disadvantage: The consequences of chronic illness*, London: Tavistock.

McLean, C. A. and Campbell, C. M. (2003) 'Locating research informants in a multi-ethnic community: ethnic identities, social networks and recruitment methods', *Ethnicity and Health*, 8, 41-62.

McLeod, A., Baker, D. and Black, M. (2006) 'Investigating the nature of formal social support provision for young mothers in a city in the North West of England', *Health and Social Care in the Community*, 14(6), 453-64.

Manning, A. and Petrongolo, B. (2005) *The part-time pay penalty*, CEP Discussion Paper No. 679, London: CEP/LSE.

Martin, J. and White, A. (1987) *The financial circumstances of disabled people*, London: HMSO.

Matthews, A. and Truscott, P. (1990) *Disability, household income and expenditure: A follow-up survey of disabled adults in the Family Resources Survey*, London: HMSO.

Mirza, H. and Sheridan, A.M. (2003) *Multiple identity and access to health: The experience of black and minority ethnic women*, Working Paper Series No. 10, London: Equal Opportunities Commission.

Modood, T. (1988) "'Black', racial equality and Asian identity', *New Community*, 14, 397-404.

Modood, T. (1998) 'Anti-essentialism, multiculturalism and the 'recognition' of religious groups', *The Journal of Political Philosophy*, 6, 378-99.

Modood, T., Berthoud, R., Lakey, J., Nazroo, J., Smith, P., Virdee, S. and Beishon, S. (1997) *Ethnic minorities in Britain: Diversity and disadvantage*, London: PSI.

Molloy, D., Knight, T. and Woodfield, K. (2003) *Diversity in disability: Exploring the interactions between disability, ethnicity, age, gender and sexuality*, DWP Research Report No. 188, London: The Stationery Office.

Montgomery, J.D. (1991) 'Social networks and labour-market outcomes: toward an economic analysis', *The American Economic Review*, 81(5), 1408-18.

Mutchler, J.E., Burr, J.A., Massagli, M.P. and Pienta, A. (1999) 'Work transitions and health in later life', *Journals of Gerontology Series B: Psychological Sciences and Social Sciences*, 54(5), S252-61.

NACAB (National Association of Citizens Advice Bureaux) (1991) *Barriers to benefit: Black claimants and social security*, London: NACAB.

NACAB (1996) 'Failing the test', *Benefits*, April/May, 19-20.

Nazroo, J. and O'Connor, W. (2002) 'Idioms of mental distress', in W. O'Connor and J. Nazroo (eds) *Ethnic differences in the context and experience of psychiatric illness: A qualitative study (EDCEPI)*, London: Department of Health, 29-40.

Njobvu, P., Hunt, I., Pope, D. and McFarlane, G. (1999) 'Pain amongst ethnic minority groups of South Asian origin in the United Kingdom: a review', *Rheumatology*, 38, 1184-7.

Nolan, M., Grant, G. and Keady, J. (1996) *Understanding family care: A multidimensional model of caring and coping*, Buckingham: Open University Press.

Olsen, W. and Walby, S. (2004) *Modelling gender pay gaps*, EOC Working Paper Series No. 17, Manchester: Equal Opportunities Commission.

Parker, G. (1993) *With this body: Caring and disability in marriage*, Buckingham: Open University Press.

Peach, C. (ed) (1996) *Ethnicity in the 1991 Census, Volume 2: The ethnic minority populations of Great Britain*, London: HMSO.

Platt, L. (2002) *Parallel lives? Poverty among ethnic minority groups in Britain*, London: Child Poverty Action Group.

Platt, L. (2003) 'Social security in a multi-ethnic society', in J. Millar (ed) *Understanding social security: Issues for policy and practice*, Bristol: The Policy Press, 255-76.

Platt, L. (2006) *The ethnic pay gap for men and women*, Manchester: Equal Opportunities Commission.

Pudney, S., Hancock, R. and Sutherland, H. (2004) *Simulating the reform of means-tested benefits with endogenous take-up and claim costs*, Working Paper No. 2004-04, Colchester: Institute for Social and Economic Research, University of Essex.

Room, G. (2000) 'Trajectories of social exclusion: the wider context for the third and first worlds', in D. Gordon and P. Townsend (eds) *Breadline Europe: The measurement of poverty*, Bristol: The Policy Press, 407-39.

Scharf, T., Phillipson, C., Smith, A. E. and Kingston, P. (2002) *Growing older in socially deprived areas: Social exclusion in later life*, London: Help the Aged.

Sharpe, L. and Curran, L. (2006) 'Understanding the process of adjustment to illness', *Social Science and Medicine*, 62, 1153-66.

Shaw, A., Walker, R., Ashworth, K., Jenkins, S. and Middleton, S. (1996) *Moving off Income Support: Barriers and bridges*, Department of Social Security Research Report No. 53: London: HMSO.

Sherbourne, C.D., Meredith, L.S., Rogers, W. and Ware, J.E. Jr (1992) 'Social support and stressful life events: age differences in their effects on health-related quality of life among the chronically ill', *Quality of Life Research*, 1, 235-46.

Sixsmith, J. and Boneham, M. (2002) 'Men and masculinities: stories of health and social capital', in C. Swann and A. Morgan (eds) *Social capital for health: Insights from qualitative research*, London: Health Development Agency.

Smaje, C. (1996) 'The ethnic patterning of health: new directions for theory and research', *Sociology of Health and Illness*, 18, 139-71.

Smith, A. and Twomey, B. (2002) 'Labour market experiences of people with disabilities', *Labour Market Trends*, August, 415-27.

Smith, N., Middleton, S., Ashton-Brooks, K., Cox, L. and Dobson, B. with Reith, L. (2004) *Disabled people's costs of living: More than you would think*, York: Joseph Rowntree Foundation.

Swain, J., French, S., Barnes, C. and Thomas, C. (eds) (2004) *Disabling barriers: Enabling environments* (2nd edition), London: Sage Publications.

Townsend, P. (1979) *Poverty in the United Kingdom: A survey of household resources and standards of living*, London: Penguin.

TUC (Trades Union Congress) (2005) *Countering an urban legend: Sicknote Britain?*, London: TUC.

Ville, I. (2005) 'Biographical work and returning to employment following spinal cord injury', *Sociology of Health & Illness*, 27(3), 324-50.

Ville, I. and Guerin-Pace, F. (2005) 'Identity in question: the development of a survey in France', *Population-E*, 60, 231-58.

Ville, I., Ravaud, J.F., Diard, C. and Paicheler, H. (1994) 'Self-representations and physical impairment: a social constructionist approach', *Sociology of Health & Illness*, 16, 301-21.

Vogt, T.M., Mullooly, J.P., Ernst, D., Pope, C.R. and Hollis, J.F. (1992) 'Social networks as predictors of ischemic heart disease, cancer, stroke and hypertension: incidence, survival and mortality', *Journal of Clinical Epidemiology*, 45(6), 659-66.

Wayne, N. (2003) *Out of sight: Race inequality in the benefits system*, London: Disability Alliance.

Whelan, C.T. (1993) 'The role of social support in mediating the impact of economic stress', *Sociology of Health & Illness*, 15(1), 86-101.

Williams, G. (1984) 'The genesis of chronic illness: narrative construction', *Sociology of Health & Illness*, 6, 174-200.

Wood, G.D. and Salway, S. (2000) 'Policy arena introduction: securing livelihoods in Dhaka slums', *Journal of International Development*, 12, 707-22.

Young, H., Grundy, E. and Jitlal, M. (2006) *Care providers, care receivers: A longitudinal perspective,* York: Joseph Rowntree Foundation.

Zaidi, A. and Burchardt, T. (2004) 'Comparing incomes when needs differ: equivalisation for the extra costs of disability in the UK', *Review of Income and Wealth*, 51(1), 89-114.

Appendix A: Qualitative fieldwork

BOX A1: QUALITATIVE WORK: PHASE ONE METHODS

Following a number of preparatory visits and meetings with numerous people living and working in the areas, a seven-day period of assessment was conducted by a team of four to six researchers. Six distinct data collection tools were employed by the team in each of the four ethnic 'communities'.

Transect walk: The research team undertook pre-planned, purposive walks through the selected areas with the aim of identifying key features of the local community and observing local people going about their everyday business. Community researchers identified suitable routes and, in some cases, local residents accompanied the research team, pointing out places of significance. This tool, together with the other tools described below, was used to complete an inventory of local resources available to community members. Two such walks were completed in each community.

Observation and informal discussions: The research team spent time chatting with people informally in places where they normally go. We visited numerous locations including mosques, churches, shops, Job Centres, travel agents, cafes and restaurants, hairdressers, community centres, workplaces, leisure centres and parks. We found many people willing to spend time with us talking about their lives. A list of topics and questions was used to guide the discussions.

Key informant interviews: Semi-structured interviews were carried out using a guideline with individuals who we identified as having particular knowledge about the community, and in particular some understanding of how longstanding health conditions may affect families. We conducted between four and ten of these interviews in each location. We talked to a wide variety of individuals including community workers, job agency staff, employers, shopkeepers, pharmacists, long-term residents, a police officer, religious teachers and school teachers.

Ethnographic interviews: Detailed, open-ended interviews were conducted with a small number of people in each of the four locations who were identified as having a long-term health condition. The focus of these interviews was on understanding the personal experiences of respondents. These interviews were tape-recorded and those that contained rich information were transcribed in full.

Small group discussions: The research team held guided discussions with small groups of men and women using two different tools: an employment matrix, which explored local job opportunities and preferences; and a problem tree, which explored the knock-on implications of long-term health conditions for families. These group discussions (at least two in each location) were arranged in mosques, churches, schools, community centres, workplaces and residents' homes.

Following the period of data collection, a two-day debriefing workshop was held for each location/community in which the research team, including the community researchers, worked together to synthesise the findings.

Table A1 provides a profile of the people with a long-term health condition who were interviewed.

Table A1: Profile of individuals with long-term health conditions interviewed in depth (N=57)

	Bangladeshi		Pakistani		Ghanaian		White English	
	Men	Women	Men	Women	Men	Women	Men	Women
Health condition[a]								
Diabetes	1	3	2	3	2	2	2	0
Depression	2	3	0	5	0	2	4	3
Heart disease	2	0	1	1	0	0	0	0
Arthritis	1	0	0	0	1	1	3	1
Joint/limb problems	1	2	1	0	0	2	2	1
Cancer	1	0	0	0	0	1	1	1
Other condition	1	3	4	2	3	1	3	2
Age group[b]								
20-29	0	1	0	1	0	1	0	1
30-39	1	4	1	2	0	0	1	1
40-49	1	1	2	3	2	2	4	3
50-59	3	2	2	2	1	4	2	1
60+	0	0	1	0	4	0	1	1
Missing	0	0	0	0	0	1	0	0
Marital status								
Currently married[c]	5	5	5	7	5	1	4	3
Divorced/separated	0	2	1	1	2	4	2	2
Widowed	0	1	0	0	0	0	0	0
Single, never married	0	0	0	0	0	2	2	2
Employment status								
Currently working	0	1	2	0	3	1	2	2
Never worked	0	4	0	5	0	0	0	0
Worked in past	5	3	4	3	2	7	7	5
Interview language not English	3	6	2	4	1	1	0	0
Family member also interviewed[d]	2	2	3	3	1	3	3	2
Total number	5	8	6	8	7	8	8	7

Notes:

[a] Health conditions are those reported by the respondents. They may or may not have been explicitly diagnosed by a health professional. The number of conditions reported is greater than the number of respondents because individuals commonly reported more than one condition. 'Other conditions' included: kidney disease (3), angina (3), high blood pressure (3), stroke (2), sight problems (2), infertility problems (1), lupus (1), Parkinson's (1), lung disease (1), loss of hearing (1), balance problems (1), muscular dystrophy (1), asthma (1), spleen problems (1), anxiety (1) glaucoma (1), and sight loss (1).

[b] One Ghanaian woman did not give her age.

[c] 'Currently married' includes those in long-term cohabiting relationships. In a few cases spouses were resident overseas but contact was maintained.

[d] A total of 29 individuals who were living with someone with a long-term health condition were also interviewed. Nineteen of these were members of the same family as individuals with long-term conditions who we had interviewed. A large number of family members also had long-term health conditions themselves.

Appendix B: Rates of ill health and caring

Figures B1 to B3 provide the context to our study by using large-scale data sources to illustrate rates of ill health. Figures B1 and B2 show the rates of ill health and caring across England and Wales, and within the areas of London that are the focus of our study, drawing on tables from the 2001 Census. Figure B1 shows that rates of long-term ill health in our study area are similar to or slightly lower than those for England and Wales, at 17-18%. However, rates of long-term ill health are closely related to age, and the average age in our study area is lower than that for England and Wales as a whole. Thus, when we restrict the comparison to people of working age we see that the rates are substantially higher in the study area, at around 10% compared with 8%. Similarly, with regard to the rates of 'not good health', which ask people to rate themselves relative to those of the same age, we find that the percentage who consider themselves to be in not good health is around 1 percentage point higher in the study area.

Figure B1: Percentage of individuals with poor health, England and Wales, London, and study area boroughs, 2001

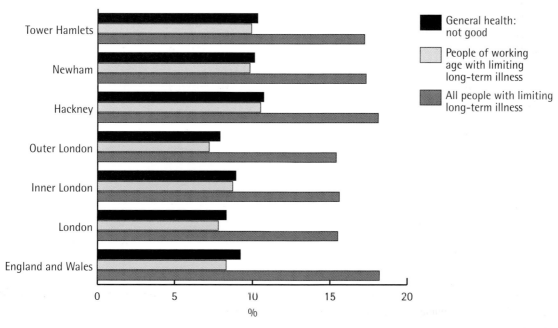

Source: 2001 Census, Crown Copyright 2003

Figure B2 shows the rates of caring across England and Wales and the study area. It shows that rates of caring are somewhat lower in the study area than in England and Wales as a whole, with between 7.5 and 8.5% of people providing some unpaid care compared with 10% overall. However, these figures have not been adjusted for age profile, and the call on unpaid care will be higher where there is a larger proportion of older people.

Figure B2: Percentage of individuals performing unpaid care, England and Wales, London and study area boroughs, 2001

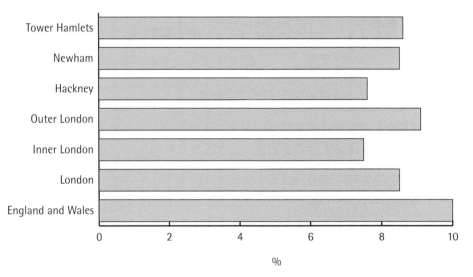

%

Source: 2001 Census, Crown Copyright 2003

Turning to look at differences by sex and ethnic group, Figures B3 and B4 show the rates of long-term ill health by ethnic group and age band (among those of working age) for men and women respectively. They show that among White British men and women, rates of ill health are broadly comparable across the age bands, although they increase steeply for men in the last five years of working age, compared to the previous five years. (This 60-64 age band is not given for women given their current earlier retirement age.) The figures also show that rates of ill health are low across all groups at younger ages, but that they start diverging by ethnicity in the 25-34 age band for women and in the 35-54 age band for men. At older ages, rates of ill health are much higher among Pakistanis and Bangladeshis, both men and women.

Figure B3: Proportion of individuals with long-term ill health, by age band and ethnic group, 2001: men

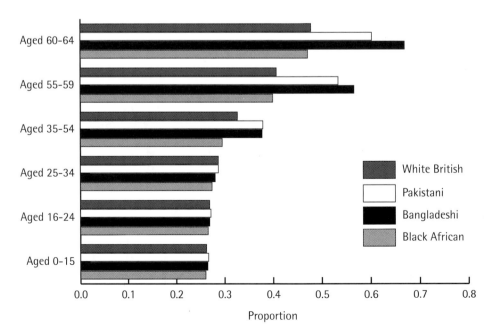

Proportion

Source: 2001 Census, Crown Copyright 2003

Figure B4: Proportion of individuals with long-term ill-health, by age band and ethnic group, 2001: women

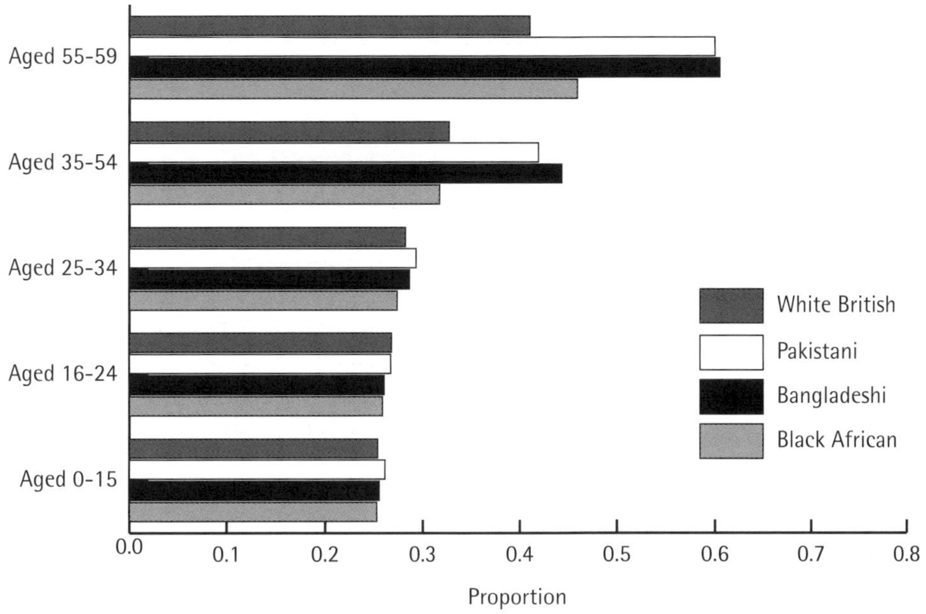

Source: 2001 Census, Crown Copyright 2003

The questions on long-term ill health used in the LFS differ from those used in the 2001 Census and allow a more fine-grained approach. We would therefore not expect the levels of ill health reported to correspond with any precision, although we find that the patterns in the LFS (shown in Chapter 2) are broadly confirmed by those in the Census.

Appendix C: Summary of DWP measures aimed at reducing the number of sickness benefit claimants

The government's Welfare Reform Green Paper (DWP, 2006a) set out a package of measures aimed at reducing the number of individuals receiving ill-health-related benefits. These included reforms to the benefit 'gateway' and to the levels of entitlement for those newly receiving such benefits. A press release from the DWP in February 2005 summarised the changes as follows:

'The key elements of benefit reforms for new claimants are:

- The name 'Incapacity Benefit' will be scrapped so that people are not immediately classed as incapable.
- Initially people will be put on a holding benefit paid at JSA [Jobseeker's Allowance] rates, accessing the new reformed benefits only once they have been through a proper medical assessment. This will take place within 12 weeks, and be accompanied by a new Employment and Support Assessment.
- Two new benefits 'Rehabilitation Support Allowance' and 'Disability and Sickness Allowance' will differentiate between those who have a severe condition and those with potentially more manageable conditions.
- The majority who have more manageable conditions will receive the 'Rehabilitation Support Allowance'. It will offer everyone a basic benefit at JSA levels (about £55), but then ensure that they can build up to get more than today's long-term IB rate by giving them extra money, first for attending Work Focused Interviews, and then also for taking steps to get them back towards the labour market.
- Those with the most severe conditions will automatically receive more money than now on the 'Disability and Sickness Allowance'. They will be able to volunteer to take up employment support.
- All of this will be built on the foundations of our successful Pathways to Work programme which is being extended to a third of the country on the road to making this a national offer'. (www.dwp.gov.uk/mediacentre/pressreleases/2005/feb/ben020205-focus.asp)